HIDDEN TREASURES

HIDDEN TREASURES

WHAT MUSEUMS CAN'T OR WON'T SHOW YOU

HARRIET BASKAS

Guilford, Connecticut

Project editor: Meredith Dias
Text design/layout: Maggie Peterson

Library of Congress Cataloging-in-Publication Data

Baskas, Harriet.
  Hidden treasures : what museums can't or won't show you / Harriet Baskas.
    pages cm
  Includes bibliographical references and index.
  ISBN 978-0-7627-8047-1
  1. Museum exhibits—United States—Miscellanea—Catalogs. 2. Curiosities and
wonders—United States—Catalogs. I. Title.
  AM11.B37 2013
  069'.5—dc23
                            2013015007

Printed in the United States of America

10 9 8 7 6 5 4 3 2 1

FOR ROSS, PARTNER IN TRAVEL, MUSEUM VISITS, AND ALL ELSE.

And in memory of my mom.
She rode along on some visits to unusual East Coast museums early on
and I wish she was around for new adventures.
And to remind me that I'm a person and not a pair of pants.

CONTENTS

Introduction   xi

Mounted (Non-radioactive) Walrus Skull—   1
Anchorage Museum (Alaska)

Psychiana Collection and Nude Mozert Painting—   4
Sedona Heritage Museum (Arizona)

Gold Jewelry—   7
San Joaquin County Historical Museum (Lodi, California)

Richard Nixon Arm Wrestling George McGovern—   10
Richard Nixon Presidential Library and Museum
(Yorba Linda, California)

Lifelike Sculptures—   13
Denver Art Museum (Colorado) /
Boca Raton Museum of Art (Florida)

A Slice of 150-Year-Old Wedding Cake—   16
P. T. Barnum Museum (Bridgeport, Connecticut)

Livingstone's Medicine Chest—   19
Wellcome Collection (London, England)

Purygin's Park of Recreation—   23
Boca Raton Museum of Art (Florida)

Saltshakers and Shrunken Heads—   25
Lightner Museum (St. Augustine, Florida)

***Shunga* (Japanese Erotica)—**   28
Honolulu Museum of Art (Hawaii)

Malvina Hoffman Sculptures—   31
The Field Museum of Natural History (Chicago, Illinois)

Matchbox Flea Diorama—   34
The Children's Museum of Indianapolis (Indiana)

Half-Heads Preserved in Jars—   37
Indiana Medical History Museum (Indianapolis)

Ball Jars Collection—   **40**
Minnetrista Heritage Collection (Muncie, Indiana)

Abraham Lincoln Pole Banner—   **43**
Wayne County Historical Museum (Richmond, Indiana)

Ghost Dance Shirt—   **46**
State of Iowa Historical Museum (Des Moines)

***In Cold Blood* Tombstones and Gallows—**   **49**
Kansas Museum of History (Topeka)

Creepy Things and Live Ammunition—   **51**
Thomas D. Clark Center for Kentucky History (Frankfort)

Spiro T. Agnew Collection—   **54**
Hornbake Library at the University of Maryland (College Park)

Masonic Urns—   **57**
Grand Lodge (Boston, Massachusetts)

Lifelike Glass Sea Life and Historically Significant Insects—   **60**
Harvard's Museums (Cambridge, Massachusetts)

Drunken Monkeys Diorama and Ford Model T Violin—   **64**
The Henry Ford (Dearborn, Michigan)

Invisible Art—   **68**
Walker Art Center (Minneapolis, Minnesota)

Truman's Portrait on the Head of a Pin—   **71**
Harry S. Truman Library and Museum (Independence, Missouri)

Human-Skin Wallets—   **74**
Museum of Osteopathic Medicine (Kirksville, Missouri)

Radiendocrinator—   **77**
National Atomic Testing Museum (Las Vegas, Nevada)

Hidden Clues in a Music Box—   **80**
Morris Museum (Morristown, New Jersey)

***Our Lady* Photo—**   **84**
Museum of International Folk Art (Santa Fe, New Mexico)

Glass Coffin—   **87**
Corning Museum of Glass (Corning, New York)

Controversial Firefighter Lithographs—   **91**
FASNY Museum of Firefighting (Hudson, New York)

The Neustadt Collection of Tiffany Glass—   **94**
Queens Museum of Art (Queens, New York)

Katharine Wright's Knickers—   **97**
International Women's Air & Space Museum (Cleveland, Ohio)

No Room for the Pig—   **100**
Rock and Roll Hall of Fame and Museum (Cleveland, Ohio)

"Old Sparky" Chair Too Uncomfortable to Exhibit—   **102**
Ohio History Center (Columbus)

John Dillinger's Gun—   **106**
Dayton History (Ohio)

Battery Notes Too Hazardous to Handle—   **109**
Chemical Heritage Foundation (Philadelphia, Pennsylvania)

Poisonous Art—   **112**
Penn Museum (Philadelphia, Pennyslvania)

Warhol Time Capsules—   **115**
Andy Warhol Museum (Pittsburgh, Pennsylvania)

Wreath from Andrew Johnson's Grave—   **118**
Andrew Johnson National Historic Site and
National Cemetery (Greenville, Tennessee)

John Murrell's Mummified Thumb—   **121**
Tennessee State Museum (Nashville)

Pottery Sherds—   **124**
Scurry County Museum (Snyder, Texas)

Coded Message in a Bottle—   **127**
The Museum of the Confederacy (Richmond, Virginia)

Smallpox Scab and Redacted Love Letter—   **130**
Virginia Historical Society (Richmond)

TSA 9/11 Artifacts—   **134**
TSA Museum (Arlington, Virginia)

Moon Boots and Space Suits—   **137**
National Air and Space Museum,
Smithsonian Institution (Washington, DC)

Condoms and Marie Curie's Radium—   **141**
National Museum of American History,
Smithsonian Institution (Washington, DC)

Repatriated Wampum—   **144**
National Museum of the American Indian
(Washington, DC, and New York City)

Soap Man—   **148**
    National Museum of Natural History,
    Smithsonian Institution (Washington, DC)

Stolen Art—   **151**
    Isabella Stewart Gardner Museum (Boston, Massachusetts)
    and Maryhill Museum of Art (Goldendale, Washington)

Barefoot Bandit Evidence—   **154**
    Orcas Island Historical Museum (Eastsound, Washington)

Rock and Roll Artifacts—   **158**
    EMP Museum (Seattle, Washington)

Swastika and KKK Quilts—   **161**
    Yakima Valley Museum (Washington)

Harley-Davidson Beer, Wine Coolers, and Cigarettes—   **165**
    Harley-Davidson Museum (Milwaukee, Wisconsin)

Acknowledgments   **169**

Index   **171**

About the Author   **176**

INTRODUCTION

My interest—okay, my obsession—with telling the stories of objects that museums rarely or never show to the public began many years ago while I was visiting a small community museum in a rural Oregon town.

I was already producing radio stories about unusual museums and having a great time visiting with people around the country who had amassed the world's largest collections of everything from lightbulbs and Barbie dolls to mechanical musical instruments, bad art, bananas, and nuts. Then, assigned to create a guidebook listing all of the museums (unusual or not) in the Pacific Northwest, I decided to make a personal visit to as many as I could find.

What I learned right away is that when you are the only guest in a small museum that doesn't get many out-of-town visitors, the volunteer on duty is apt to follow you around. Sometimes it's due to a mistrust of outsiders. More often it's simply because it's nice to have a curious visitor—or any visitor—come through the front door.

Partly to be polite, and partly because I'm just a nosy person, I'd often ask my museum "minder" to tell me about his or her favorite things on exhibit. That way I would usually learn about a local treasure I might have otherwise overlooked, and I didn't have to feel so uncomfortable having someone following me around. At the end of one of these tours, my guide lowered her voice, looked around furtively (even though no one else was in the museum), and said, "If you think that's interesting, you should see what they keep locked away in the back room."

Right away, I wanted to see what was back there. Then, of course, I wanted to know what was in the back room at every museum. And then I needed to find out why so many museums keep some really great stuff locked away in the vaults.

That led to the twenty-six-part *Hidden Museum Treasures* radio project that aired over several years on National Public Radio, to a variety of other "What's in the back room?" projects, and now, to this book.

And while it is titled *Hidden Treasures,* this not an investigative, tell-all report on what I found out about secret societies of museum employees, board members, and historians who meet late at night in dark corners of the storage rooms to box up and lock away batches of important objects you and I will never get to see.

The main reason most museums rarely or never display some very significant and intriguing objects is actually sort of boring: From the smallest community museum to the largest branch of the Smithsonian Institution, at most museums there's just barely enough room to display more than 5 or 10 percent of their holdings at any one time. And space isn't the only issue: A lot of great things stay tucked away because they are just too old, too fragile, or too likely to be ruined by exposure to humidity and to light. And museums are in the business of keeping things safe and intact for a long time.

But what I discovered is that there are plenty of other surprising, thought-provoking, alarming, and even funny reasons that, for example, a collection of condoms, a six-hundred–pound glass coffin, a portrait of former vice president Spiro Agnew made out of feathers, a 150-year-old piece of cake from Tom Thumb's wedding, a giant inflatable pig, and a certain pair of knickers remain in storage rooms around the country. And why a wallet made out of human cadaver skin and a creepy-looking doll named "Jimmy" aren't likely to be put on display anytime soon.

It turns out that some objects are kept from view because they are too political or too culturally sensitive to be on exhibit. Others are considered too valuable, some you can't see because they have been stolen, and in the case of a wee bit of radium that belonged to two-time Nobel Prize winner Marie Curie now at the Smithsonian Institution's National Museum of American History, some objects are simply too hot or too dangerous to handle.

Curious? Before you turn the page and start looking at all the great photos of hidden treasures that museums around the country generously shared with me for this project, a few disclaimers are in order.

My home-base state of Washington is well represented here because I know a lot of the museum "secrets" in my own backyard. And while I've included the story of two unusual quilts from the Yakima Valley Museum (one has a connection to the Ku Klux Klan; one doesn't, but which one may be a surprise) and the story of the two missing peace medals handed out by Meriwether Lewis and William Clark when their expedition passed through this territory, I had to leave out the story of the 150-year-old pickle now kept in a refrigerator at the Lynden Pioneer Museum near Bellingham and the century-old piece of bread discovered at the Lopez Island Historical Society and Museum because my "really old food" quota had already been met by entries from other states.

There are multiple entries in these pages from museums in Ohio and Indiana as well. The museum communities in those states seem to be especially well organized and well endowed with hidden treasures. And when my call for nominations for this book hit the Internet they responded with gusto, with great stories, and with objects that range from medical specimens and a diorama made with flea heads to the electric chair known as "Old Sparky" and a gun that belonged to John Dillinger, the Depression-era bank robber who was declared Public Enemy #1.

The Smithsonian Institution weighs in heavily here as well, by way of rarely or never seen objects from its vast collection of more than 137 million artifacts. Included are the stories behind repatriated wampum from the National Museum of the American Indian, lunar boots and Neil Armstrong's iconic spacesuit from the National Air and Space Museum, condoms and that sample of Marie Curie's radium from the National Museum of American History, and a fellow known as "Soapman" whose body resides in a special storage area at the National Museum of Natural History.

Last-minute entries include the story of the TSA Museum in Arlington, Virginia, which collects and displays many items relating to the awful, terrifying events of September 11, 2001, and its aftermath, but is off-limits to the general public. And although it is another Washington state–centered story, I squeezed in an entry about the community of Orcas Island, Washington, which in late 2012 began debating whether it would be appropriate for the local museum to accept and display evidence from the trial of Colton Harris-Moore, who became known as the Barefoot Bandit. Harris-Moore spent a lot of time on Orcas Island during a two-year crime spree that stretched from Washington state's San Juan Islands to Canada and the Bahamas and included dozens of burglaries and break-ins and the theft of cars, boats, bikes, and planes. And while, like it or not, the story is now part of local history, some residents would rather not have their local museum add to the convicted criminal's notoriety.

For a book all about the stories behind what's tucked away in museum storage areas, I was disappointed that I was unable to secure images for some objects with very compelling stories.

In Spokane, Washington, the small Crosbyana Room at the entrance of the Crosby Student Center at Gonzaga University serves as a museum for exhibiting about two hundred Bing Crosby–related items, including gold and platinum records, awards, memorabilia, and some unusual objects, such as the mousetrap that the Crosby Research Foundation invented. Scrapbooks, records, cassettes, disks of Crosby's many radio shows, and thousands of other items from the world's largest Bing Crosby collection are stored in the special collections vault in the university's Foley Center Library. And one of those items is a box containing several toupees that belonged to and were worn by the well-known singer and actor.

Although Crosby wasn't shy or secretive about the fact that his contract with the movie companies required him to wear hairpieces in some of his movies (he called them "hair doilies"), the library has been told that some members of Crosby's family are. So the library would not share a photo of those toupees with me for this project.

Due to a standing court order, ongoing litigation, and issues relating to the Native American Graves Protection and Repatriation Act of 1990 (NAGPRA), the Bishop Museum in Honolulu, Hawaii, was unable to discuss or share images of the sacred and culturally important objects involved in a long-running and complex custody battle over items that were removed from the Kawaihae Caves complex (also known as Forbes Cave) on the Island of Hawaii in 1905 by David Forbes, an amateur archaeologist and curio collector. Forbes eventually sold or gave most of the objects to the museum and while no one has been arguing about whether human remains Forbes dug up should be reburied, up to a dozen local groups have been debating whether objects such as a very detailed, carved, two- to three-foot-tall figure of a woman with human hair and mother-of-pearl inserts for her eyes "want" to be seen or whether the objects need to be reburied in the cave to set things right.

And the Mattatuck Museum, in Waterbury, Connecticut, was ultimately uncomfortable sharing images of Fortune, a man who had been enslaved to a local doctor in the late 1700s and whose skeleton had been displayed at the museum for many years with the name "Larry" inscribed on his head.

The skeleton had been removed from exhibit in 1970, but in the mid-1990s, Fortune's true identity and life story began to be pieced together when Waterbury's African-American History Project Committee decided to begin its research on local black history with that skeleton locked in the museum basement.

Today the museum has a permanent exhibit about Fortune, and about slavery, with videos of the skeleton being examined, a facial reconstruction based on Fortune's skull that was created by a noted forensic artist, and a painting done by a medical illustrator showing what Fortune may have looked like when he was alive. And after years of community discussion and debate about whether Fortune's bones should continue to be studied or given a respectful burial, as this book was going to press, plans were in place for Fortune's bones to be laid to rest in a local cemetery.

While I'm truly disappointed at not being able to include these stories with the rest of the hidden treasures in this book, for me they further underscore the fact that sometimes the issues around what gets displayed and what stays in storage can get very complicated and contentious for communities and for museums.

While I still can't tour a museum's galleries without wondering what they've got tucked away in storage, I have come to agree with Ken Arnold, head of public programs at the Wellcome Collection in London, which can display only a very small but, for me, always intoxicating selection from Henry Wellcome's collection of more than 1.5 million books, objects, and artifacts relating to the history and practice of medicine around the world.

"One of the great myths of the museum world is that we should perpetually strive to put as much of our collections on show for as long as we can," says Arnold. "My sense instead is that one of the most important roles of the museum is precisely the opposite: namely to keep safe material that is off display and at rest, so that it can then be rediscovered and reinterpreted afresh when it has had a chance, if you like, to recharge its batteries."

Here then, are the stories behind more than fifty museum treasures that have been recharging their batteries for years.

MOUNTED (NON-RADIOACTIVE) WALRUS SKULL

Anchorage Museum (Alaska)

Alaska's Anchorage Museum celebrates the state's history, science, art, and Alaska Native culture with a core collection of more than twenty-five thousand objects ranging from early whaleboats and rare Alaska Native artifacts to a section of the trans-Alaska oil pipeline and a moon rock collected during the 1971 Apollo 15 mission.

The fifteen-thousand-square-foot Alaska Gallery employs more than one thousand objects, as well as full-scale and miniature dioramas, to explore the history and ethnology of the country's forty-ninth state. Seven galleries, including one devoted entirely to the work of Sydney Laurence, Alaska's best-known artist, display art that reflects Alaska and the circumpolar North. And in a special arrangement with the Smithsonian Institution, more than six hundred indigenous Alaska artifacts and culturally important treasures held for many years outside the state in the Smithsonian's collection have been returned to their place of origin and are displayed in an impressive multimedia gallery that includes artifact exhibits, videos, oral history recordings, and natural sounds from the Alaskan environment.

Now a world-class museum that ranks high among the top ten most visited Alaskan attractions, the Anchorage Museum had humble beginnings. When it first opened its doors back in 1968, the museum displayed just sixty borrowed paintings featuring scenes of Alaska, and it had a collection consisting of fewer than three thousand objects on loan from another institution.

Even before the museum had its own building, portions of the collection were being exhibited in a downtown municipal building. And that's where, for a very short time, visitors in 1966 might have seen the mounted walrus skull in this picture (page 3).

"During the 1950s and '60s this was a very common, quintessentially Alaskan item," says Monica Shah, director of collections/chief conservator of the Anchorage Museum at Rasmuson Center. "At the time, this was a very collectible item in Alaska. People would take the entire skull, mount it on a plaque made of wood, and hang it on the wall. The one we have here was made as a floor stand."

Shah says while the Anchorage Museum does not focus on natural history (the Anchorage Museum of Natural History does that), it does have some taxidermy bear, moose, musk ox, walrus tusks, and other animal specimens that it uses to complement and improve other exhibits; however, this walrus skull stays in storage.

Labeled in 1965 by the original donor as the "First Known Alaskan Atomic Victim," the skull is said to be from one of one hundred walruses that washed up on a beach in 1953 near Cape Newenham, a promontory jutting out between Bristol Bay and Kuskokwim Bay, on the Bering Sea. The word back then was that the walruses died as a result of atomic testing being conducted by Russia off the Siberian coast.

Exhibited briefly in 1966, along with the label connecting it to an atomic test, the skull was put away when concerns were raised over its possibly being radioactive. "Visitors were taken aback that we would display something like that and at least one museum visitor left the premises immediately after reading the label," says Shah.

The skull stayed in storage until 2000 and would have stayed off exhibit had not a guest curator spotted it on the shelves and asked to include it in an exhibit. But before permission could be given, the skull was sent out to be tested for radioactivity. None was found and the skull was included in a three-month temporary show.

Since then, the mounted walrus skull has remained in storage. "We all like him and think of him as kind of a collections standby," says Shah. "And while some of us used to think that the old, original label was a joke, we realize now that many of the details do add up."

Anchorage Museum at Rasmuson Center
625 C St.
Anchorage, AK 99501
(907) 929-9200
www.anchoragemuseum.org

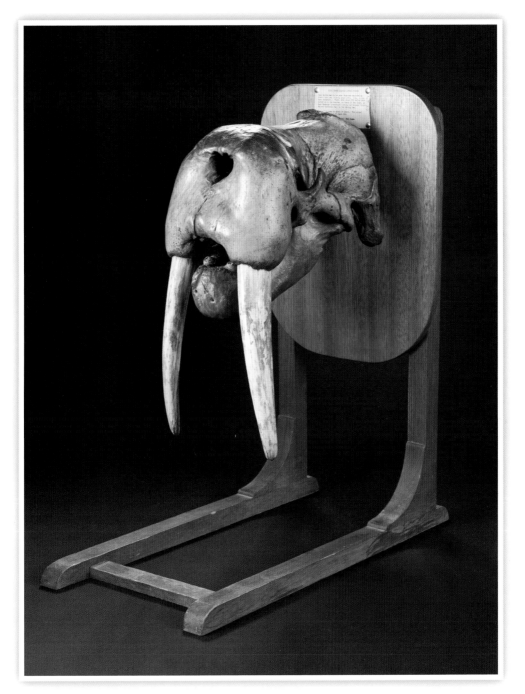

Exhibited briefly in 1966, this walrus skull was put away over concerns that it was radioactive. It's not. MOUNTED WALRUS SKULL, ANCHORAGE MUSEUM COLLECTION, 1965.22.1

PSYCHIANA COLLECTION AND NUDE MOZERT PAINTING

Sedona Heritage Museum (Arizona)

Homesteaders began settling the area around what is now known as Sedona, Arizona, in the late 1800s and, beginning with the 1923 film *Call of the Canyon*—based on Zane Grey's novel by the same name—the area's impressive red-rock formations became a familiar backdrop for many of Hollywood's most successful, star-studded westerns.

Artists, writers, and later, seekers of spirituality and healing found their way to Sedona, and today tours to local sacred sites and vortexes of "enhanced energy" are offered alongside a plethora of places to get massages, spa treatments, hypnotherapy, and all manner of alternative healing.

Sedona didn't become a full-blown New Age mecca until the 1980s, but it turns out at least one local citizen subscribed—literally—to an unusual alternative religion back in the 1930s.

Janeen Trevillyan, historian for the Sedona Heritage Museum, says that in 2008 the museum received cases of material that once belonged to John Franklin Thompson, a noted local citizen whose father was the area's first homesteader, in 1876. Volunteers cataloging Thompson's papers discovered several large, thick envelopes filled with pamphlets and brochures related to Psychiana, a now-forgotten alternative religious movement invented in 1928 by Frank B. Robinson, who distributed his "lessons" to subscriber-members via mail until his death in 1948.

"Robinson had developed a positive-thinking theology," explains American spiritual history expert Mitch Horowitz, "that was similar to others bubbling up at the time." Horowitz says Robinson's success—he claimed to have as many as two million subscribers—was due not only to the fact that he married his ideas to the scientific and psychological language of the time, but that he was a brilliant marketer. "He took out ads in newspapers and magazines. The most famous ad read, 'I talked with God. Yes I did. And you can too. It's easy!' People accused him of being a P. T. Barnum figure, but on the brink of the Great Depression, ads like this spoke to people's needs," says Horowitz.

Among the Psychiana-related items now at the Sedona Heritage Museum is a button bearing an image of Adolf Hitler. During the early days of World War II, Robinson mailed buttons like this to his subscribers, urging them to join him in a prayer crusade to bring victory to the Allied forces. The vow that accompanied the button read: "I am helping to bring Hitler's defeat by repeating hourly: the power of Right (God) will bring your speedy downfall."

Pinup painter Zoë Mozert gave this self-portrait to the Sedona Heritage Museum. SEDONA HERITAGE MUSEUM, SEDONA ARIZONA

Sedona Heritage Museum historian Trevillyan says that while it's quite interesting, the Hitler pin has never been put on display because "we find that anything related to Hitler is a lightning-rod topic for many people," and that as a small, volunteer-run organization, "we have to be careful about doing something that can be considered controversial."

Some of the museum's Psychiana materials are cataloged on the museum's website, but Trevillyan says the museum staff hasn't quite figured out how to put together an exhibit. "It's easy to find basic information about the movement on the Internet," she says. "The harder part would be figuring out how to explain how it reached this area and that farmer at a time when the town barely had reliable postal service and had only recently established its first church."

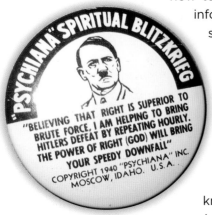

Subscribers to Psychiana, a now-forgotten religious movement, were mailed this button during World War II and asked to pray for Adolf Hitler's downfall. SEDONA HERITAGE MUSEUM, SEDONA ARIZONA

The reason the museum doesn't display what it believes is a self-portrait of artist and former resident Zoë Mozert is simpler for Trevillyan to explain. Mozert was a model and well-known illustrator who created hundreds of paintings and magazine covers featuring Hollywood starlets and pinup girls, and among her most famous works is the poster for the controversial Howard Hughes film *The Outlaw*, starring Jane Russell.

"Naked is the problem," says Trevillyan. "We're a small, family-oriented museum, and how in the world are we ever going to show it? We laugh sometimes and say if we ever have an art exhibit, we'll have to put that painting in a separate room, behind a black curtain."

Sedona Heritage Museum
735 Jordan Rd.
Sedona, AZ 86336
(928) 282-7038
http://sedonamuseum.org

Sources include: Mitch Horowitz, "The Mail-Order Prophet," *Science of Mind Magazine*, March 2007.

GOLD JEWELRY

San Joaquin County Historical Museum
(Lodi, California)

At its 18.5-acre campus in Lodi, California, near Stockton, the San Joaquin County Historical Museum keeps watch over more than fifty thousand historic items representative of the region's history.

Displays throughout the eight exhibition buildings tell the stories of the original Native American inhabitants of the region (the Yokuts and the Miwok) and of the area's earliest settlers, as well as the history of grape growing, winemaking, ranching, farming, and other local and historical industries. There's also room for exhibits of tractors and other agricultural equipment as well as examples of earthmoving and leveling equipment. In an exhibit hall devoted to horse-drawn transportation, there's a restored peddler's wagon that's been stocked with pens, pencils, paper, cufflinks, pots, pans, and other items offered by an early traveling salesman along a route that ran between Stockton and the foothill towns of the Sierra Nevada prior to the railroads.

Four relocated and preserved historic buildings, including the one-room Calaveras schoolhouse (1866) and the Charles Weber Cottage (1847), are also on museum property. That cottage, one of the earliest structures built in what is now the city of Stockton, was the home of Captain Charles M. Weber, the town's founder and first farmer. During the gold rush of the early 1850s, Weber dabbled in mining, but history books note that he was savvy enough to realize there was more reliable profit to be made from selling tools and provisions to others heading out with dreams of finding gold and striking it rich.

Weber obviously got his hands on some gold, though, because among the many objects that have come to the museum from his descendants is an exquisite set of jewelry that includes a necklace, a choker, a brooch, a bracelet, and earrings made of gold, with freshwater pearls and diamonds. According to museum collections and exhibit manager Julie Blood, the Weber family believes the town's founder gave this set to his wife, Helen Murphy-Weber, as a wedding gift in 1850. "The jewelry is made from eighteen-karat gold with a twenty-four-karat gold overlay," says Blood, "and is said to have been made from some of the first gold found in California. The pearls are said to be from Baja California."

Gold jewelry belonging to Helen Murphy-Weber, wife of Captain Charles M. Weber, founder of Stockton, California, is too valuable to display. CHARLES M. WEBER FAMILY COLLECTION, SAN JOAQUIN COUNTY HISTORICAL SOCIETY

As you can see, the jewelry set is breathtaking. But it's a sight few museum visitors get to see due to some very real concerns about security. Museum officials are just not confident they have an exhibit case secure enough to protect this treasure—a situation that is, unfortunately, not unusual in the world of community museums.

"There have been several incidents noted in the media where museums or historic sites have been targeted for gold specimens on display," says Blood. "So the jewelry is only taken out for special occasions, meetings, and presentations and is then secured in a vault that is monitored and guarded closely at all times. The museum does not see the situation changing anytime in the near future."

Among the incidents that make museum officials extremely cautious about displaying these gold treasures is the daring daylight theft that took place on a Friday afternoon in late September 2012 at the California State Mining and Mineral Museum, a unit of the California State Parks, in Mariposa, less than one hundred miles away.

According to news reports, two men wearing face masks and night goggles—and armed with pickaxes—ran into the museum, herded the two employees on site that afternoon to one end of the building, and then made off with gold and precious gems worth more than $2 million. Officials suspect the treasure the thieves were really after was the museum's main and most valuable attraction: an impressive mass of crystalline gold from the gold-rush era that weighs nearly fourteen pounds and is known as the Fricot Nugget. When the thieves tried to grab the nugget from its spot in the museum's vault, alarms were triggered and that hefty hunk of gold remained unharmed.

San Joaquin County Historical Society & Museum
Micke Grove Regional Park
11793 N. Micke Grove Rd.
Lodi, CA 95240
(209) 331-2055
www.sanjoaquinhistory.org

RICHARD NIXON ARM WRESTLING GEORGE MCGOVERN

Richard Nixon Presidential Library and Museum
(Yorba Linda, California)

Richard Milhous Nixon, the thirty-seventh president of the United States, was among the country's most controversial commanders-in-chief and the only US president (so far) to resign from the office. He served as vice president from 1953 to 1961 and during a not-quite-two-term presidency (1969–1974) visited and initiated diplomatic relations with the People's Republic of China, signed the Strategic Arms Limitation Treaty with the Soviet Union (1972) and legislation abolishing the military draft (1971), met with Elvis Presley at the White House (1970), and signed the Paris Peace Accords (1973), which ended American involvement in the Vietnam War.

These and any other of his accomplishments remain forever overshadowed by the Watergate scandal, which began with the news of a break-in at the Democratic National Committee offices in Washington, DC, in June 1972 and spread to include a wide array of crimes, cover-ups, secret White House tape recordings, and on August 8, 1974, Nixon's announcement that he would resign from the presidency the next day. (Then–vice president Gerald Ford stepped in to replace Nixon. And on September 8, 1974, Ford pardoned the former president for "all offenses against the United States.")

After leaving office, President Nixon struck a deal with the General Services Administration that might have allowed him to destroy presidential and other materials that he claimed were his personal property. That included thousands of photographs, broadcasts, video and audio tapes (including the secretly recorded "White House tapes"), forty-six million pages of documents, and more than thirty thousand gifts from foreign heads of state and American citizens, including a diamond watch from the defense minister of Saudi Arabia, an official painting of St. Peter's Basilica from Pope Paul VI, a painting of Nixon done on black velvet, another on corduroy, and yet another that depicts him as a gladiator.

Congress and two decades of litigation succeeded in saving all those materials, and the collection now resides at the nine-acre Richard Nixon

Presidential Library and Museum in Yorba Linda, California, which also includes the house in which Nixon was born, his grave site, and Army One, a helicopter used by Presidents Kennedy, Johnson, Nixon, and Ford and the one that whisked Nixon away from the White House on August 9, 1974, the day he resigned from office.

Many artifacts from the collection are used in the permanent and temporary exhibits in the museum, but supervisory museum curator Olivia Anastasiadis says a few items seem destined to stay forever tucked away in storage.

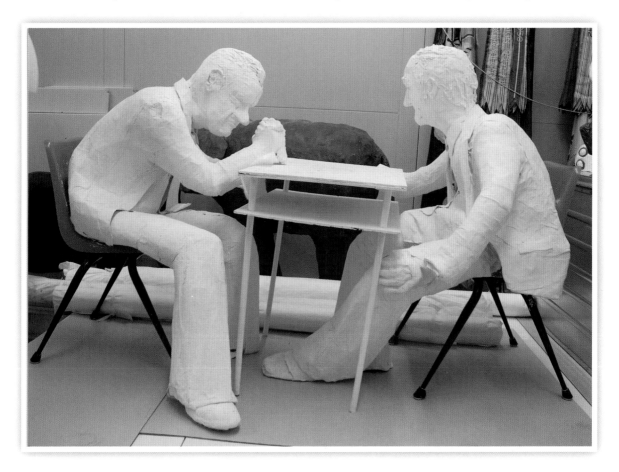

This plaster and papier-mache statue shows President Richard Nixon (left) and his 1972 electoral opponent, Senator George McGovern, arm-wrestling. It was made by art students at Lancaster Country Day School in Pennsylvania but is now damaged. IN THE COLLECTIONS OF THE RICHARD NIXON PRESIDENTIAL LIBRARY AND MUSEUM, NARA. MADE BY STUDENTS AT THE LANCASTER COUNTRY DAY SCHOOL, 1972. PHOTOGRAPHED BY STAFF AT THE NIXON LIBRARY.

One such item is a giant clam given to President and Mrs. Nixon on October 26, 1969, by the Philippine ambassador, His Excellency Ernesto V. Lagdameo, and Mrs. Lagdameo. "It obviously represents the Philippines' natural resources," says Anastasiadis, "but the valve has collapsed and needs a mount to 'stretch' it in place inside the shell. That's a difficult conservation project and, at six hundred pounds, this clam shell is really hard to move around."

Another item stored away is one Anastasiadis considered putting on display during the *Nixon as Icon* exhibit in 2011, but the white plaster sculpture of Richard Nixon arm wrestling Senator George McGovern (Nixon's opponent in the 1972 presidential race) is damaged. "One of the feet is broken, one of the hands is cracked, and before we could display it we'd need to find funding to get a conservator to fix it," she says.

The sculpture was made in 1972 by a group of ninth-grade students at Lancaster Country Day School in Pennsylvania. They had recently visited an exhibit at the Philadelphia Museum of Art that featured the work of pop artist George Segal, who used unpainted white plaster casts of models as sculptures. Their art teacher, Mary Elizabeth Patton, says her students were inspired to try to make their own plaster bandage sculpture. Because the Nixon/McGovern presidential campaign was under way, the class decided to portray the two candidates having an arm wrestling contest. After Nixon won the election, the school's headmaster contacted the White House and a delegation of students traveled to Washington, DC, to present the sculpture to a Nixon aide for the presidential collection.

"One of my former students contacted me recently and said he thought the sculpture was probably in a dump someplace," says Patton. But she discovered that the sculpture was shipped from Washington, DC, to California along with everything else in the Nixon collection, including gifts from heads of state. And even though the work is a bit mangled, Patton says, "It's good to know it is still there—a little worse for wear, but still there."

Richard Nixon Presidential Library and Museum
18001 Yorba Linda Blvd.
Yorba Linda, CA 92886
(714) 983-9120
www.nixonlibrary.gov

LIFELIKE SCULPTURES

Denver Art Museum (Colorado) / Boca Raton Museum of Art (Florida)

The Denver Art Museum houses more than seventy thousand works of art and is best known internationally for its holdings of American Indian art and for its pre-Columbian and Spanish colonial collections. The museum's permanent collection also includes major holdings in Asian, European, and American; modern and contemporary; and western American art. But locally the museum is well known as the home of *Linda.*

The realistic sculpture arrived at the museum in 1984 and had been created a year earlier by Colorado artist John DeAndrea, a sculptor best known for his meticulously realistic polyvinyl sculptures of people, most often of women, who are entirely nude or, like *Linda,* modestly draped or clothed.

"Our members love *Linda.* She is a Denver institution that our visitors have grown up with and look forward to seeing again and again," says museum spokeswoman Kristy Bassuener.

Unfortunately, though, this very popular and asked-about work of art can be put on exhibit for only a short time every few years.

This time limitation is in place not because the museum is worried someone will try to wake up what looks like a real woman sleeping in the museum or try to cover her up but, because like a great deal of art and objects in museum collections everywhere, *Linda* is very sensitive to light.

The sculpture "is made from plastic materials that are unfortunately subject to inherent and inevitable deterioration," explains Kate Moomaw, assistant conservator of modern and contemporary art. "Deterioration of plastics typically leads to issues like color change, distortions, and increased brittleness."

Because exposure to light during an exhibition contributes significantly to deterioration, *Linda*'s time on view is rationed out and, when the sculpture is on exhibit, the museum keeps light levels in the gallery relatively low.

When not on view, *Linda* is left to sleep, undisturbed, in dark storage. But when the museum does plan an exhibition that includes *Linda,* it sends out an announcement to the community and to the museum membership alerting them to the occasion.

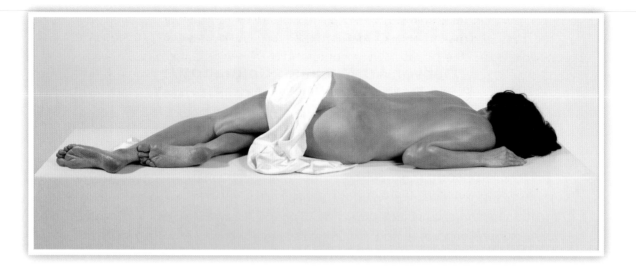

John DeAndrea's hyper-realistic polyvinyl sculpture *Linda* is very popular but only occasionally on view. JOHN DEANDREA, *LINDA*, 1983. DENVER ART MUSEUM COLLECTION: FUNDS FROM 1983 COLLECTORS CHOICE, DR. CHARLES AND LINDA HAMLIN, SHEILA BISENIUS, PHYLLIS AND ARON B. KATZ, JAN AND FREDERICK MAYER, CAROLINE AND REX. L. MORGAN, GULF OIL FOUNDATION, MARSHA AND MARVIN NAIMAN, JOEL S. ROSENBLUM, FUND, AND ANONYMOUS DONORS, 1984.1. PHOTO (C) DENVER ART MUSEUM 2012. ALL RIGHTS RESERVED.

Florida's Boca Raton Museum of Art also has a polyvinyl DeAndrea sculpture, but *Released,* created in 1989 and intended as a response to Michelangelo's *Rebellious Slave,* is unlikely to be put on view.

"Although *Released* is a simple nude sculpture, because of the hyper-real quality of the subject, she is both sufficiently sexy and tortured to exclude from any exhibitions we mount here," says museum assistant curator Kelli Bodle. "Regardless of the aesthetic merits and technical acumen of DeAndrea's work, in fact because of them, the sculpture is far too transgressive and suggestive for the many schoolchildren that visit the museum on a daily basis."

The museum did exhibit *Released* during its *Shock of the Real: Photorealism Revisited* exhibition in 2008, "but there was enough outcry over the sculpture that we removed her after two days," says Bodle.

"Yes, that happens," says artist John DeAndrea, "and it makes me terribly sad. I've been making this art for more than forty years now, trying to educate people about the beauty of the human body. My work is not about sex; it's about people. And many of them just happen to be nude."

Denver Art Museum
100 W. 14th Ave. Pkwy.
Denver, CO 80204
(720) 865-5000
www.denverartmuseum.org

Boca Raton Museum of Art
501 Plaza Real
Boca Raton, FL 33432
(561) 392-2500
www.bocamuseum.org

A SLICE OF 150-YEAR-OLD WEDDING CAKE

P. T. Barnum Museum (Bridgeport, Connecticut)

Huckster, hoaxer, showman, and above all shrewd businessman Phineas Taylor (P. T.) Barnum never actually said "There's a sucker born every minute," but he sure knew it.

According to Neil Harris, author of *Humbug: The Art of P. T. Barnum,* the impresario built his offbeat empire with the knowledge "that exposure is crucial to celebrity; that notoriety increases fame. And that behind the scenes revelations can be endlessly fascinating."

Before 1871, when he became a founding partner in the Barnum and Bailey's Circus, Barnum made a good living, and assured himself of a lively legacy, by entertaining and educating a curious and often gullible public with curiosities, marvels of nature, historic oddities, and unusual cultural and artistic exhibits and performances of all kinds at his American Museum in New York City.

The museum operated from 1842 until it burned down in 1865 (a replacement museum burned as well, in 1868) and featured on-site wax-figure and taxidermy departments, a continuous stream of performers and lecturers, and changing exhibitions ranging from automatons and live animals (including whales) to the latest and most modern devices designed to save labor and inspire wonder.

Barnum also displayed real people. His star attractions included Siamese twins Chang and Eng Bunker and Anna Swan, a giantess from Nova Scotia who was said to be at least seven and a half feet tall. And when he learned about Charles Sherwood Stratton, a young man only twenty-five inches tall, the canny promoter put him on the payroll and renamed him General Tom Thumb.

The museum grabbed headlines, and record-breaking attendance, by displaying the "original" Fejee mermaid, a man-made, half-monkey-half-fish creature that Barnum hyped by using storybook-style ocean maidens in advertisements and promotions.

In the late 1880s Barnum gave land and money to establish the Barnum Institute of Science and History in Bridgeport, Connecticut, which was completed in 1893, two years after his death.

The facility initially served as a lecture hall, library, and museum and displayed objects related to Barnum and his family, along with items such as the lantern Paul Revere may have used, a rock said to be from the stream where David killed Goliath, a fossilized footprint, wood scarred from the battle at Gettysburg, and an Egyptian mummy named Pa-Ib, which was donated to the museum by Barnum's second wife, Nancy.

Says museum registrar Melissa Houston, "Anything unusual, old, or international was an 'oddity' in the mid-nineteenth century because people did not have the wealth or opportunity to travel and so much was unknown about the world."

Sadly, a tornado on June 24, 2010, seriously damaged what is now the Barnum Museum, but plans are under way to reopen at least part of the facility sometime in 2014. When it does reopen, many cultural and historical oddities from the collection will likely not be displayed, including a slice of cake that tells the story of Tom Thumb and Lavinia Warren, both performers in Barnum's American Museum.

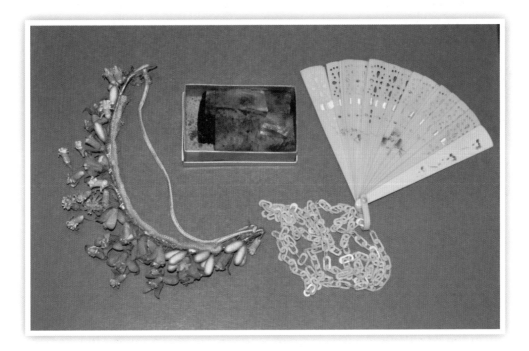

A piece of cake (center) and some accessories from the wedding of Tom Thumb and Lavinia Warren in 1863. PHOTOGRAPH COURTESY OF THE BARNUM MUSEUM

"Their 1863 wedding was a welcome respite in the newspapers from the horrors of the Civil War," says Houston, who notes that the event "made front-page news and was a little spark of hope and joy in the otherwise trouble-some war years."

The museum's collection has long included documents, lithographs, and wedding attire from the event, but a slice of boxed wedding cake in the museum's collection was not donated to the museum until 2000.

The cake is still in its small box and, because it is a fruit cake soaked (most likely) in brandy, it has been well preserved, though shrunken from its original size.

"It was common to give guests a small slice as a memento of the wedding, and presumably it was to be eaten a year later. That didn't happen with this piece, which was given to a Connecticut guest and passed down in the family until it was donated to the museum," says Adrienne Saint-Pierre, museum collections manager.

Why is it not on display?

"Like other artifacts of this type, it could rapidly deteriorate if exposed to light for too long," says Saint-Pierre. "And frankly, most visitors would have a hard time understanding that this dark, hard-looking but sparkly-from-sugar item is actually a piece of 150-year-old wedding cake."

P. T. Barnum Museum
820 Main St.
Bridgeport, CT 06604
(203) 331-1104
www.barnum-museum.org

Sources include: Barnum Museum staff, Barnum Museum website, and "P. T. Barnum," a lecture by Neil Harris, author of *Humbug: The Art of P. T. Barnum,* April 24, 2012. Chappell Great Lives Lecture Series at the University of Mary Washington, Fredericksburg, Virginia.

LIVINGSTONE'S MEDICINE CHEST

Wellcome Collection (London, England)

London's Wellcome Collection bills itself as a "destination for the incurably curious," and anyone who visits this unusual museum will find a venue humming with programs and events designed to illustrate and explore "the connections between medicine, life and art in the past, the present and the future."

In addition to temporary exhibitions that have covered everything from the medical and cultural significance of hearts and brains to the art and science of sleep and the iconography of death, the museum has several permanent exhibitions, including one that displays an eclectic and extraordinary cross section of items collected by Henry Wellcome, the museum's namesake.

Wellcome was born in Wisconsin, grew up in Minnesota, and made his fortune in England as a pharmaceutical entrepreneur and cofounder (in 1880) of Burroughs Wellcome & Co. The company made its mark (and its many millions) by being the first to introduce compressed medicine tablets in Britain and by trademarking the brand name Tabloid.

Not only was Wellcome a savvy businessman, he was also a voracious and intensely inquisitive collector. When he died in 1936, he left behind more than 1.5 million books, objects, and artifacts, most of them relating to the history and practice of medicine around the world.

When it came to collecting, Wellcome was very inclusive. Highlights on display from his collection range from diagnostic dolls and healing amulets to Japanese sex aids, artificial eyes, Napoleon's toothbrush, a mummified body, and what is thought to be a lock of King George III's hair. Other treasures on display include a shrunken head, Charles Darwin's whalebone and ivory walking stick, and fine art and paintings depicting alchemists, doctors, pharmacists, and virgins.

As with many other museums in London and elsewhere, the Wellcome Collection has many more artifacts than it can ever put on display in its galleries. And among the items in storage are, of course, some intriguing objects that have rarely or never been seen by the public.

For example, while the museum does display a frightening torture chair from the collection, there's a storeroom full of torture implements tucked away at London's Science Museum, which is the custodian for a large amount of Henry Wellcome's vast collection.

Special exhibitions offer an opportunity to bring out unique objects from storage. And in 2011, as part of a unique collaboration called *First Time Out,*

Explorer Algot Lange took this medicine chest on his 1911 Amazon expedition. It is one of the rarely seen treasures in the Wellcome Collection. WELLCOME IMAGES

one of the Wellcome Collection's (tamer) hidden treasures was displayed for a short time in five London-area museums.

For that show, five major local institutions—the Wellcome Collection, the Horniman Museum, the Natural History Museum, the Science Museum, and the Royal Botanic Gardens, Kew—each chose one previously unseen item from their archives and displayed it for the first time. In the exhibition, each object was on display at each of the participating institutions for six weeks, and at each institution the object's descriptive label was reinterpreted from the special perspective of that museum.

For the special exhibition, the Horniman Museum, home to more than 350,000 objects in three collections spanning natural history, anthropology, and musical instruments, took an Easter Island (Rapa Nui) dance paddle out of storage. The Natural History Museum brought out the cranium and mandible of an extinct giant lemur. The Royal Botanic Gardens, Kew, displayed Japanese botanical art painted on the wood of the trees represented and framed in their bark. And the Science Museum brought out a tray of small toys used by noted English child psychologist and psychotherapist Margaret Lowenfeld (1890–1973).

The Wellcome Collection plucked Livingstone's Medicine Chest from storage. The leather chest, which evoked the name of the famous explorer David Livingstone (of "Dr. Livingstone, I presume" fame), was supplied by Burroughs Wellcome & Co. to the Swedish-American explorer Algot Lange for use during his 1911 Amazon expedition. When it was displayed at the Wellcome Collection, the exhibit notes said in part, "Commonly advertised as 'Livingstone's Medicine Chest,' these compact cases were featured in all the major expeditions of the time. Bearing the marks of use acquired during these heroic undertakings, the cases were then returned to the company and displayed at international fairs in dioramas that mimicked contemporary museums of natural history and ethnography."

Museum visitors learned a bit more about Lange and his exploits when the case was put on display at London's Science Museum. There, exhibit notes explained that "Lange's published account of his travels contained excruciatingly detailed descriptions of his various medical complaints" and of his claims to have "encountered cannibals, a 50-foot anaconda and vast quantities of gold," which he unfortunately neglected to bring home "because he was too ill to carry it."

Ken Arnold, the Wellcome Collection's head of public programs, says the "deliciously small-scale project" provided a great opportunity for each participating museum, and for members of the public, to learn a great deal about objects that had never before been put on view. For the Wellcome, "it also allowed us to uncover the medical significance of four other objects originally collected by naturalists, botanists, historians, and ethnographers, held by partner institutions in the project. And this collaborative curiosity turned five stored objects into twenty-five exhibits," says Arnold.

In fact, the carousel-style *First Time Out* exhibition of hidden treasures was so successful that the participating museums have agreed to delve into their storage rooms, retrieve more hidden treasures, and do it again.

Wellcome Collection
183 Euston Rd.
London NW1 2BE, United Kingdom
+44 (0) 20 7611 2222
www.wellcomecollection.org

PURYGIN'S PARK OF RECREATION

Boca Raton Museum of Art (Florida)

Major collections at Florida's Boca Raton Museum of Art include European paintings and sculptures from 1775 to 1945, modern and contemporary art from the 1960s to the present, American art, photography, decorative art, paintings, drawings, West African tribal and Oceanic art, and other items. The museum also has two gardens filled with public art and sculptures by many noted artists.

With short-term exhibitions that have explored everything from video games and miniature golf to quilts with political messages, it's fair to say the museum is not shy about exploring art's nooks and crannies and beckoning a wide range of visitors inside the front door.

Officials at the Boca Raton Museum of Art try to keep young children from seeing the explicit *Purygin's Park of Recreation*. LEONID PURYGIN (RUSSIAN, 1951–1996), *PURYGIN'S PARK OF RECREATION*, 1989, OIL ON CANVAS, 72X78 INCHES. BOCA RATON MUSEUM OF ART, PERMANENT COLLECTION. 1996.021. GIFT OF MS. HARRIET GOLDER.

But while the museum offers many special events and activities for families and is delighted to welcome the busloads of students who come by for field trips, there's at least one painting the staff has tucked away in hopes that young children won't see it.

The painting is called *Purygin's Park of Recreation* and was created by Russian artist Leonid Anatolievich Purygin (1951–1996).

Museum assistant curator Kelli Bodle notes that Purygin made this painting in 1989, three years before the Union of Soviet Socialist Republics (USSR) collapsed. She says the title of the painting references a line from the Soviet Constitution of 1936 (also known as the "Stalin Constitution") that reads "Citizens of the USSR have the right to rest and leisure."

In this painting, "Purygin reveals the fallacy behind the decree," says Bodle. "He shows plentiful vodka and sausage as gifts to the workingmen and -women of Russia who accept the spoils of the communist government while still forced to live in terror amongst KGB agents. Piles of decapitated heads reference Stalin's purges and executions. Sodomy and violence proliferate against the dark background and Purygin includes a self-portrait in the center as a range target, awaiting death."

Bodle says the museum is proud to display Purygin's "vehement disavowal of Stalin's power regime," as preserving the way in which artists interpret war is an important role for a museum. But she says that the museum also must pay careful attention to the audience that visits the museum and ensure that "sexually explicit platforms are not readily visible to the busloads of children visiting on field trips who might not be so closely monitored."

So while the painting of this odd pleasure playground isn't actually locked away, the museum has it "discreetly placed" and on display only for those who know where to look. "We like to keep it tucked away, hanging in the hallway that leads to the second-floor curatorial offices. Those offices are separate from the larger block of administrative offices and away from the main thoroughfare of the museum," says Bodle. "*Purygin's Park of Recreation* is still accessible to the general public, if you're willing to poke your head around a corner—which is, of course, what children love to do."

Boca Raton Museum of Art
501 Plaza Real
Boca Raton, FL 33432
(561) 392-2500
www.bocamuseum.org

SALTSHAKERS AND SHRUNKEN HEADS

Lightner Museum (St. Augustine, Florida)

Costumes, furnishings, decorative art, mechanical musical instruments, stained glass from the studio of Louis Comfort Tiffany, and other treasures from the vast collection of the Lightner Museum are exhibited on three floors of the former Alcazar Hotel in St. Augustine, Florida. The opulent resort, which opened in 1887 and closed in 1932, was designed by Carrère and Hastings, the architectural firm that also designed the Ponce de Leon Hotel across the street for wealthy industrialist Henry Flagler.

The Alcazar's Spanish Renaissance revival–style building was purchased in 1946 by Chicago publisher Otto C. Lightner, who had moved to Florida for his health and needed a place to display his vast collection of Victorian-era art and furniture.

The museum opened in 1948 and today has a Victorian Science and Industry Room that displays shells, rocks, minerals, Native American artifacts, a small mummy, and a wide variety of other curious objects. There's also a music room where some of the antique mechanical instruments "perform" daily, and exhibits that include exquisite porcelain, art glass, fine art, furniture, and other objects from the Victorian era.

Lightner (who is buried in the museum's courtyard) was the publisher of *Hobbies,* a magazine that first hit the stands in 1931, and a big believer in the power of collecting. "He thought it made you a better person, built character, and gave you a purpose," says Robert Harper, executive director of the Lightner

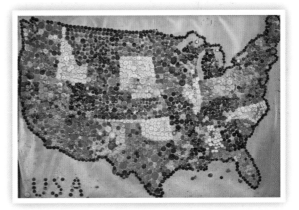

This button map of the United States shows only a fraction of the millions of buttons in the Lightner Museum's collection. "We lost part of Georgia the other day when we were moving it," jokes the museum's executive director, Robert Harper. THE LIGHTNER MUSEUM

The Lightner Museum's crowded back rooms brim with collections of everyday objects, like these saltshakers. THE LIGHTNER MUSEUM

Museum. And what you collected didn't really seem to matter. "Lightner let people know that you didn't have to be a Vanderbilt or a Fricke to be a collector," says Harper. "Collecting things such as matchbooks, salt and pepper shakers, buttons, and walking sticks was just fine."

Lightner didn't just encourage people to choose hobbies and become collectors; he encouraged them to donate their collections to his museum, which was originally called the Lightner Museum of Hobbies. That's why exhibits at the Lightner still include displays of everything from old toasters and walking canes to salt and pepper shakers and beaded purses.

Harper, who remembers going to the museum as a child and following yellow footprints painted on the floor around the courtyard into rooms filled with everything from buttons to stamps, says today the museum keeps many of the donated collections and the "really bizarre artifacts" in storage.

That includes a collection of furniture made from animal horns, about one thousand walking canes, and a jar containing a piece of cake from President Grover Cleveland's wedding that Harper says is "just too ugly" to display. He also says that most of the six thousand sets of salt and pepper shakers donated to the museum by two or three enthusiastic collectors are kept in storage because they would take up a lot of room in an exhibit and "are just not that interesting to have out all the time."

Jars and jars of what may be millions of buttons are also tucked away, as is some of the artwork made from buttons, including a fragile button map that was sewn onto a piece of inexpensive muslin. "We lost part of Georgia the other day when we were moving it," says Harper.

And then there are the shrunken heads. The museum's collection includes three shrunken heads but only one is kept on display. "When it comes to shrunken heads, one seems to be enough," says Harper. "Plus, one of the shrunken heads we have is really very gross and gruesome looking and we're just a bit uncomfortable putting it out."

Although so many collections remain in storage, the museum continues to take in some donated items. "I think the Smithsonian Institution has run out of space," says Harper, "so we've picked up the challenge."

Lightner Museum
75 King St.
St. Augustine, FL 32084
(904) 824-2874
www.lightnermuseum.org

SHUNGA (JAPANESE EROTICA)

Honolulu Museum of Art (Hawaii)

The permanent collection at the Honolulu Museum of Art contains more than fifty thousand works, including what is considered the most important Asian art collection in the country. Other collections include European and American paintings, prints, and drawings, Hawaiian art and objects, and an extensive and significant collection of textiles that includes more than six thousand works from more than sixty countries.

The museum's collection of nearly twelve thousand *ukiyo-e* ("pictures of a floating world") Japanese woodblock prints is considered one of the best of its kind in the world. Portraying images of landscapes and nature, actors, theater, and life's simple and sensual pleasures, the collection ranges from Buddhist prints that are hundreds of years old to prints made by the top artists of the twentieth century.

More than five thousand of the woodblock prints at the museum come from the collection of novelist James A. Michener, who wrote *Hawaii* and *Tales of the South Pacific*. Michener, who began collecting Japanese prints in the 1950s, wrote articles and books about them, including the well-known *The Floating World* (1954). "Michener was not a trained art historian," says Shawn Eichman, the museum's curator of Asian art. "But he definitely popularized the genre."

Due to the fragility of all the prints and their sensitivity to light, only twenty or thirty examples from the overall woodblock print collection are put on display in the museum at any one time, and these are changed out about every two months. But there's a subset of the collection that until recently had never seen the light of day due to the graphic nature of the work and taboos about showing erotica in a museum.

Called *shunga* ("spring pictures"), this form of Japanese erotica developed during the seventeenth and eighteenth centuries and "while there are very explicit images of people in sexual acts," says museum director Stephan Jost, "the work includes parody, social commentary, and how-to manuals for newlyweds that in many cases take the art beyond just visual titillation." And there was no shame in making *shunga*; major Japanese artists of the day created and signed some of the work. "It's not as if it was a separate group of artists making *shunga,*" says Jost. "It would have been as if Monet was also making erotic art."

Along with other Japanese woodblock prints and woodblock-printed books and paintings, James Michener had some *shunga* in his collection. But it seems he was skeptical about its importance to the understanding of Japanese art and Japanese aesthetics. "In his most famous book on Japanese prints, Michener dedicates a whole chapter to *shunga,*" says Eichman. "But it's a very denigrating chapter. He called them 'the other books,' and doesn't even recognize *shunga* as a category unto itself." Yet, ironically, Eichmann and others say the thirty or so works of *shunga* Michener gave to the Honolulu Museum of Art with the rest of his collection are considered among the finest examples of the genre.

Taboos about displaying *shunga,* Japanese erotic art, kept a valuable collection tucked away for years. SUZUKI HARUNOBU (1725?-1770) *SEXUAL MISCONDUCT* FROM THE BOOK *FASHIONABLE, LUSTY MANE'EMON (FŪRYŪ ENSHOKU MANE'EMON)* JAPAN, EDO PERIOD (1615-1868), 1770 WOODBLOCK-PRINTED BOOK; INK AND COLOR ON PAPER GIFT OF JAMES A. MICHENER, 1991 (24672) HONOLULU MUSEUM OF ART

Eichman says that for more than fifty years no one at the museum really wanted to display or even pay attention to the *shunga,* due to the explicit nature of the subject matter and because, like Michener, few researchers considered *shunga* of much value. "But when you cut through the excuses and the justifications," says Eichman, "I think people just weren't comfortable with the subject matter and they came up with other justifications for not dealing with it."

The way *shunga* was treated in Japan no doubt also had something to do with keeping the work out of view of the rest of the world.

Eichman explains that until the 1990s, *shunga* fell under the same Japanese law as contemporary pornography and was illegal to reproduce, even in articles about art history. "That attitude spilled outside of the boundaries of Japan proper to everyone else dealing with Japanese art as well," he says.

During the 1990s, however, there was a significant shift in how the Japanese government decided to deal with *shunga.* And while the laws didn't change, Eichman says, a "*shunga* boom" was created when the government decided to ease up on enforcing the laws as far as historical materials were concerned. Although no *shunga* exhibitions came about, in Japan many books, articles, and images relating to *shunga* were suddenly available.

And in 2003, a sort of "tipping point" was reached at the Honolulu Art Museum when Michener's collection of *shunga* was joined by eight hundred works from the collection of noted *shunga* scholar Richard Lane, an American who had lived in Japan and worked aggressively to convince the Japanese government to allow the works to be reproduced.

Eichman says the museum went back and forth for a long time trying to decide whether there would be too much negative public reaction to an exhibition of *shunga.* But the staff and the board finally decided to give it a try. And instead of putting out just a little *shunga* to see how people reacted to it, the museum decided to do three major *shunga* exhibitions, on various themes, that began in November 2012 and will continue through 2015.

"It's not for everyone," says Eichman. "And we have a separate door that makes it very clear that the subject matter is explicit. But the very fact that there's a question about whether or not to show them is really the strongest argument for why it's necessary to do an exhibition."

Honolulu Museum of Art
900 S. Beretania St.
Honolulu, HI 96814
(808) 532-8700
http://honolulumuseum.org

MALVINA HOFFMAN SCULPTURES

The Field Museum of Natural History (Chicago, Illinois)

In addition to being the home to numerous dinosaurs, including "Sue," the forty-two-foot-long, thirteen-foot-tall (just to the hip), and most complete Tyrannosaurus rex ever found, the Field Museum of Natural History in Chicago, Illinois, has a thirteen-thousand–year–old skeleton ("Magdalenian Girl"), one of the country's largest mummy collections, and a hall of gems with more than six hundred gemstones and 150 pieces of jewelry that has as its core the Tiffany & Co. Collection first displayed at the World's Columbian Exposition held in Chicago in 1893.

Drawing on a collection that includes more than twenty million specimens, the museum offers visitors a wide variety of temporary and permanent exhibits that explore anthropology, botany, geology, and zoology. Visitors can learn about Africa and its man-eating Tsavo lions, the history of China told through 450 precious jade objects, the ancient Americas, and the natural history of many other cultures and places around the world.

As in other museums, when scientists and researchers discover new things, exhibits and exhibit labeling at the Field Museum is updated and changed. In the case of the anthropological sculptures in the Field Museum's *Races of Mankind* display, changing beliefs about race led an entire exhibit to be dismantled.

The Field Museum first opened in 1921 and just eight years later, in 1929, the board commissioned artist Malvina Hoffman (1885–1966) to sculpt and cast what became a series of 104 busts, heads, and life-size figures of people from around the world. At the time many anthropologists—and curators at the Field Museum—believed there to be more than one hundred different races (some counted more than 150), and Hoffman's assignment was to depict those many races in sculptures to be installed in a hall called "The Races of Mankind" that would be the museum's entry for "A Century of Progress International Exposition," the World's Fair held in Chicago in 1933.

"At the time there was no consensus on race," says Alaka Wali, the Field Museum's curator of North America anthropology. "Many saw race as a biological category of difference or variation and they basically tried to create these typologies of the different races. The curators of the Field Museum were of the camp that thought there were many, many types of race—not just the four major types—and that's what was ultimately portrayed in this hall."

Hoffman, who had studied with the noted French sculptor Auguste Rodin (best known today for his bronze sculpture called *The Thinker* and a marble sculpture known as *The Kiss*), traveled around the world to do research and to make models and bronze casts of men and women she chose to serve as the representative "types." And although most sculptures were of individuals she met in her travels, they were labeled with generic titles such as "Australian bushman," "Chinese coolie," and "Eskimo female."

Wali says the sculptures became quite popular with Field Museum visitors, as much for their art as for their exoticness, but by the early 1940s anthropologists knew this depiction of racial types and categorization was not accurate.

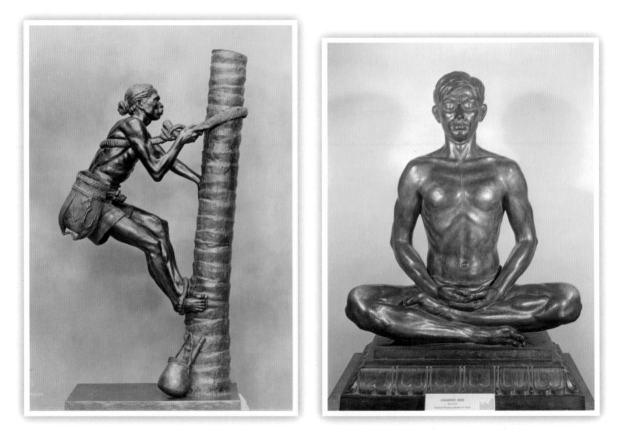

The Field Museum dismantled its *Races of Mankind* exhibit of sculptures by Malvina Hoffman due to changing beliefs about race. © THE FIELD MUSEUM

"It was not reflecting what human physical variation is all about," she says, "but the museum didn't change how they presented it or thought about it."

That change didn't happen until the 1960s, with the impetus of the civil rights movement and the dialogue about race that went on in the United States. "By then anthropologists realized they could no longer represent race this way," says Wali, "and the museum knew that it had to change that hall."

At first they tried changing the name of the hall from "The Races of Mankind" to "Portraits of Mankind," but in 1966 the decision was made to simply disassemble the exhibit entirely.

Wali and others have mixed feelings about the sculptures themselves and about the museum's decision to put them away. "The irony for me is that what Hoffman did was subvert the race project. She made bronze casts instead of the plaster sculptures the anthropologists initially wanted. She met people, molded them and sculpted their likeness, and saw them as individuals. In many of the sculptures there's a lot of individual personality that comes through."

Wali says the sculptures still have a dedicated, if somewhat complicated, following. "There's a huge affection for them. People are attracted to the sculptures for their art, the beauty of the bronze, and for Hoffman's artistry. And many people remember coming to the museum and seeing the sculptures. We get letters asking why they are not visible."

Due in part to that affection and their historic role in the museum, a dozen or so of the Hoffman sculptures are on display in the mezzanine galleries and in a few other places in the museum. But they're there as art rather than anthropological type specimens and are offered without much context.

"The sculptures themselves are very powerful and it's possible that at some point they will be used to tell a different story about race," says Wali, "the story we know now about the complexity of human variation, how scientists and laypeople have thought about race, and how that view has changed over time."

The Field Museum of Natural History
1400 S. Lake Shore Dr.
Chicago, IL 60605
(312) 922-9410
http://fieldmuseum.org

MATCHBOX FLEA DIORAMA

The Children's Museum of Indianapolis (Indiana)

Today The Children's Museum of Indianapolis has eleven galleries and a collection of more than 120,000 artifacts exploring science, culture, history, and the arts. But when the museum was first established back in 1925, its creators put notices in the local paper asking children and their families to donate artifacts and objects they thought belonged in a kid-oriented museum.

That's how a pair of snowshoes, a coverlet, and a porcupine fish that museum chief conservator Christy O'Grady says "looks pretty horrible at this point" came to be among the museum's first few accessioned items.

Since then hundreds of thousands of other toys, dolls, comic books, train sets, articles of clothing, and cultural objects relating to children and childhood have become part of the museum's permanent collection. Much of it is available to touch, play on, and explore in the five floors of what is now the world's largest children's museum—a building that's big enough to display everything from Barbie dolls and dinosaur fossils to an operating forty-two-animal Dentzel carousel from 1917; a thirty-five-foot-long, fifty-five-ton steam locomotive built in 1868; and a Conestoga wagon dating back to 1803.

But as big as the museum is, there are some treasures most visitors never get to see.

Due to concerns about fading colors in the fabric, the museum rarely displays a red "flying" cape actor Christopher Reeve wore in the filming of *Superman* and *Superman II.* Nor does it keep on exhibit the now very fragile Civil War–era drum used by Edward Black, a young boy who was just eight years old in July 1861 when he joined the Union army. The Indiana-born Black was a drummer boy for the First Regiment, 21st Indiana Volunteers, and is believed to be the youngest soldier ever to fight in the US Army.

One other rarely displayed treasure at The Children's Museum of Indianapolis is about the size of a matchbox.

In fact, it is a matchbox.

The cover of the four-inch-long matchbox is decorated with a picture of three horses, and inside the matchbox is a hazelnut shell that has been cut in half. A diorama of a tiny village has been built inside the hazelnut shell, complete with tiny figures whose tiny heads come from fleas.

The Children's Museum of Indianapolis rarely exhibits the Civil War–era drum used by Edward Black, who was just eight years old when he joined the Union army. © 2012 THE CHILDREN'S MUSEUM OF INDIANAPOLIS; PHOTOGRAPH BY WENDY KAVENY

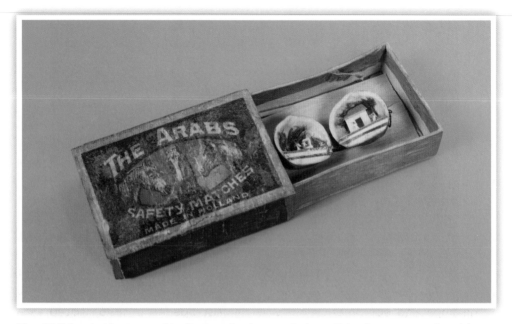

The Children's Museum of Indianapolis does not show this diorama made with fleas because it is too small for families to gather around. © 2012 THE CHILDREN'S MUSEUM OF INDIANAPOLIS; PHOTOGRAPH BY WENDY KAVENY

Museum chief conservator O'Grady explains that at one time it was popular for folk artists and, for some reason, nuns in Mexico to create miniature scenes populated with dressed fleas—*pulgas vestidas*—for the tourist trade. "Fleas dressed in wedding attire were sometimes given as wedding presents to a bride and groom," she says.

Since its donation to the museum back in 1955, this flea diorama has spent all but six weeks in storage. When on display, it sat in a specially made case set at a kid's eye level alongside a greatly enlarged photo of the open matchbox. "It's truly tiny," says O'Grady. "The main reason we keep it in storage is because people would have to line up just to see it and it would be difficult for a family to view it all together."

The Children's Museum of Indianapolis
3000 N. Meridian St.
Indianapolis, IN 46208
(317) 334-3322
www.childrensmuseum.org

HALF-HEADS PRESERVED IN JARS

Indiana Medical History Museum (Indianapolis)

The official word is that the Indiana Medical History Museum in Indianapolis is not haunted, but even some staff members admit that the building can feel sort of creepy, what with all the jars of brains and body parts around.

Adding to the creepiness is the fact that the museum is housed in what is the oldest surviving pathology facility in the country and is on the now-abandoned grounds of Central State Hospital, which opened in 1848 as the Indiana Hospital for the Insane.

The hospital remained open until 1994, but the Pathological Department Building, which still contains almost all of the original nineteenth-century furnishings and equipment from when it first opened in 1896, closed as a laboratory in 1968. The nineteen-room building opened as a museum a year later, and tours through the clinical laboratories, teaching amphitheater, and autopsy and records rooms are now offered to visitors who are interested in learning the history of the facility and the story of early scientific psychiatry and its contribution to modern medicine.

Tours begin in the surgical amphitheater and include stops in the former autopsy room, the records room, and a room called the "Anatomical Museum." That room originally served as a place where medical students and practicing physicians gathered to learn about the physical causes of mental diseases that were studied in the building, and many specimens taken from patients autopsied in the building are now displayed in this room. "There are a couple of hearts, a giant stomach, and a section of a liver," says Sarah Halter, director of public programs, "as well as two headless skeletons, some anatomical models, and a spinal column. But most are from the museum's collection of more than four hundred brain specimens."

Next to each jar on display is a note that has been transcribed from that patient's autopsy with some of the information early pathologists thought students should know. Some of the notes are very clinical, but some give details and tell a bit of the story of why someone was committed to the hospital. "There was one man who was kicked in the head by a horse when he was a child and another man who was shot in the head during the Spanish Civil War and ended up in the hospital here," says Halter.

While the museum displays hundreds of artifacts, Halter says there are many items the museum rarely or never displays. That includes patient artwork, all but one of the very fragile books filled with patient autopsy records, films of patients taken with a 16mm movie camera purchased in 1929, and autopsy and other photographs of former patients.

In addition to some quack medicines, an iron lung, and some other large pieces of equipment, the museum also keeps some unusual surgical and medical instruments used in the mid- to late 1800s tucked away, including an amputation kit, a crude stomach pump that doubled as an enema device, and dental tools that include tooth keys used to twist teeth out of a patient's mouth. "Some of these can't be displayed because of their controversial

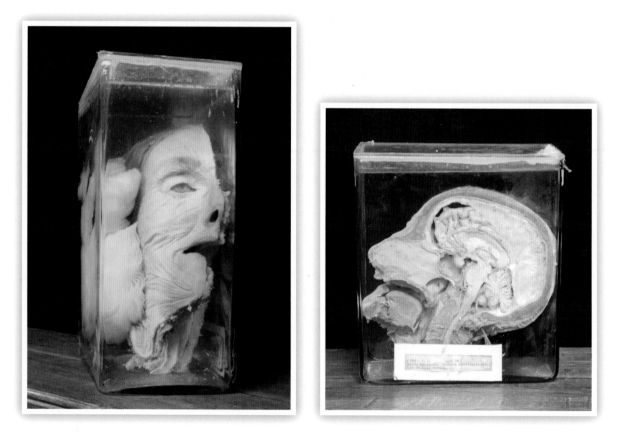

Some anatomical artifacts at the Indiana Medical History Museum in Indianapolis are not displayed due to legal and ethical reasons. INDIANA MEDICAL HISTORY MUSEUM, INDIANAPOLIS

nature," says Halter. "Some can't be displayed for legal reasons, others can't be shown for ethical reasons, and some of these items can't be displayed because there's just no room."

The museum also rarely displays two hemi-heads from 1929 that are in jars in the anatomical collection. (Originally preserved in formaldehyde liquid, they are now in formalin, a solution with a lower percentage of formaldehyde gas.) "They are exactly what they sound like: half-heads," says Halter. "Both are from female patients in their seventies who were autopsied within a month or two of each other and the remains of one of the women are buried on what once were the hospital grounds."

On one of the heads, which has been split down the middle, part of a face stares out from inside the jar. "On one side she has a face and she looks at you and she has beautiful brown hair that has been preserved," says Halter. "The brain and other internal features of the head are visible on the other side. On the other hemi-head, a lot of the skin was removed and they also cut off the top of the skull so the brain is exposed, which makes it more disturbing."

Halter says the hemi-heads are kept out of view in part because seeing them is very disturbing to some visitors. "People who are not disturbed by the heads may be there just out of a morbid interest," she says. "And we really try to stress that what they were doing here was serious scientific research. These were real people with real emotions and real problems."

Indiana Medical History Museum
3045 W. Vermont St.
Indianapolis, IN 46222
(317) 635-7329
www.imhm.org

BALL JARS COLLECTION

Minnetrista Heritage Collection (Muncie, Indiana)

In 1887 the Ball brothers—Edmund, Frank, George, Lucius, and William—moved the Ball Brothers Glass Company from Buffalo, New York, to Muncie, Indiana, to take advantage of natural gas reserves and other easy-to-access raw materials needed in the production of their best-known product: glass home-canning jars.

The company's product line and interests have changed considerably since then. The Ball logo still appears on canning jars, but the Ball Corporation got out of the glass-making business in 1996. It now makes metal packaging products and—through its Ball Aerospace & Technologies Corporation—instruments and vehicles used in space.

The company moved its headquarters to Colorado in 1998, but a decade earlier the Ball family established a museum focusing on nature, history, gardens, and art for east-central Indiana called Minnetrista (the name means "a gathering place by the water") on forty acres of land long owned by the family in Muncie.

Minnetrista's Heritage Collection includes about eight hundred glass canning jars from a collection started by George, the youngest of the Ball brothers. "He squirreled away jars that included samples of different models, mistakes, and jars others sent to him," says Karen Vincent, Minnetrista's director of collections. After George's death in 1955, the company continued the tradition of collecting jars and eventually set up a small museum at corporate headquarters that was visited mostly by employees and those who stopped by on business.

Since 1998, when the jar collection moved to Minnetrista, most of the jars have stayed in storage. And except for a temporary exhibit that included a few hundred jars, only a dozen or so are on display at any one time.

That means few have seen the fragile six-foot-long canes and other "whimsies" workers in the glass factory made after hours, the Centennial Jars, the Tomb of the Dead Canary, or the canned space tomatoes.

The Centennial Jar collection is made up of two one-gallon jars and one four-gallon jar originally exhibited in Philadelphia in 1876 at the Centennial International Exhibition, the first official World's Fair held in the United States.

Vincent points out that these aren't Ball jars, which weren't manufactured until 1884, but says they were part of George Ball's original jar collection and still contain food, "probably pears that you can see in the dark liquid." The jars are "incredibly heavy" and Vincent says they're rarely put on view because "if something broke, it would be a heck of a mess."

The jar containing a long-dead canary became part of the collection in the 1950s. Vincent explains that probably back in the 1930s, a family wrapped its deceased pet canary in a cloth, put it in a Ball jar, and buried it in their backyard. At a reunion many years later, some family members dug up the jar and discovered that it looked much the same as the day they'd buried it. "In the 1950s they sent their beloved pet in the jar to Ball brothers for safekeeping," says Vincent.

Minnetrista's jar of space tomatoes contains tomatoes grown from seeds that were sent into space in 1984 as part of the "Seeds in Space" partnership between NASA and the Park Seed Company. The seeds spent five years in orbit and, after they were retrieved and returned to Earth, were planted by schoolchildren around the world. Students at Burtsfield Elementary School in

A deceased pet canary, wrapped in cloth and buried in a Ball jar, was dug up at a family reunion and brought to the Minnetrista Heritage Collection for safekeeping. MINNETRISTA HERITAGE COLLECTION, MUNCIE, INDIANA

West Lafayette, Indiana, grew these space tomatoes and preserved them in jars donated by the Ball Corporation.

These jars contain tomatoes grown from seeds that were sent into space.
MINNETRISTA HERITAGE COLLECTION, MUNCIE, INDIANA

Minnetrista
1200 N. Minnetrista Pkwy.
Muncie, IN 47303
(765) 282-4848 or (800) 428-5887
www.minnetrista.net

ABRAHAM LINCOLN POLE BANNER

Wayne County Historical Museum (Richmond, Indiana)

Founded in 1929 in part to house the vast collection of art and cultural objects that wealthy society matron Julia Meek Gaar had picked up in her world travels, the Wayne County Historical Museum in Richmond, Indiana, has grown to include eight exhibit buildings and thousands of artifacts. Exhibits today include everything from an Egyptian mummy, horse-drawn carriages, historic automobiles, and a Conestoga wagon to dolls, dollhouses, and a wide variety of Native American artifacts.

Many items in the museum's vast holdings came to the museum around 1930, shortly after the museum was founded. And with no professional staff or good record-keeping system, objects from those early days were often not properly identified. "Someone might have called a piece of crystal a glass jar," says museum director James Harlan, "or overlooked important details about an object."

That "come one, come all" approach applied to paintings as well. And Harlan says the museum currently has a storage room filled with artwork, much of it from the 1830s to 1860s, for which there is scant documentation. "They didn't take photographs of the paintings. And many were unsigned. But they'd take a painting, put it on a shelf, and then put another painting on top of it. Soon you have a shelf with fifty to one hundred oil paintings and not much information about any of them."

Mislabeling is a common way for treasures to end up lost or "hidden" inside museum collections, as another Indiana museum, the Evansville Museum of Arts, History, and Science, learned in early 2012. A painting the museum had stored in an old shipping crate for forty years turned out to be *Seated Woman with Red Hat,* a work by Pablo Picasso estimated to be worth between $30 million and $40 million.

A somewhat less valuable but equally exciting discovery was made at the Wayne County Historical Museum when a woman called to make an appointment to photograph a flag her grandmother had donated to the collection more than thirty-five years ago. "I pulled out the box the flag was stored in and when we began unfolding the flag we discovered it wasn't just a flag," says Harlan. Instead it was a rare and very valuable flaglike banner, eight feet

This valuable banner used to campaign for Abraham Lincoln in 1860 was mislabeled and "lost" when put in storage. WAYNE COUNTY HISTORICAL MUSEUM, RICHMOND, INDIANA

by ten feet, used to campaign for Abraham Lincoln and his running mate, Hannibal Hamlin, in 1860.

"People would support their candidate by making the largest banner possible and raising it on the tallest pole they could find," says Harlan. Not only was the banner a rare find, but inside the box was a handwritten note telling of the five local women who had hand-sewn the banner and raised it for the election. "Needless to say, I was speechless. We've since researched the women and their husbands, had the banner conserved by an expert, and put it on display at the museum for a short time," he says.

Then there are the items Harlan would like to display but can't, such as weapons and jewelry that are suspected to be stolen "and things we've been told we have but I can't find. Supposedly there's a bat here signed by Babe Ruth, but I haven't seen it."

Wayne County Historical Museum
1150 N. A St.
Richmond, IN 47374
(765) 962-5756
http://waynecountyhistoricalmuseum.com

GHOST DANCE SHIRT

State of Iowa Historical Museum (Des Moines)

One of Daniel Boone's guns, a lock of George Washington's hair, horse collars from the world's largest and smallest horses, Civil War battle flags, and fuel rods from a 1950s nuclear reactor at Iowa State University are among the more than 100,000 artifacts in the collection of the State Historical Society of Iowa, the organization that oversees the State Historical Museum and has been collecting material remains of Iowa's past since 1857.

A commercial photographer from Chadron, Nebraska, got to the scene of the Wounded Knee massacre to record the carnage shown here. STATE HISTORICAL SOCIETY OF IOWA

These items, along with vintage aircraft, Native American artifacts, fossils, and dioramas depicting Iowa's wildlife have all been on display over the years at various times in the museum, but state curator Jerome Thompson says there are some items the museum rarely or never displays due to incomplete documentation and cultural sensitivities.

Both of those issues come into play in the case of a buckskin shirt that has been in the collection since the early 1900s.

Thompson says early collection records link the shirt to the Wounded Knee massacre, which took place at Wounded Knee Creek in South Dakota on December 29, 1890. On that cold day, the US Army's Seventh Cavalry surrounded and eventually killed what is estimated to have been up to three hundred unarmed men, women, and children of the Lakota Sioux on the Pine Ridge Reservation. Many of the tribal members had been followers of a nonviolent movement that believed an Indian messiah would soon arrive. The sacred Ghost Dance, performed while wearing special clothing, was one of the rituals performed as part of that movement.

In 1995, not long after the passage of NAGPRA, the Native American Graves Protection and Repatriation Act, the museum inventoried its holdings to determine if there were Native American cultural items, such as human remains, funerary objects, sacred objects, or objects of cultural patrimony, that needed to be returned to descendants or culturally affiliated Indian tribes in the region. Thompson and a researcher from the Cheyenne River Sioux Tribe examined the buckskin shirt and noticed that it is painted as opposed to beaded and that it was cut at the seams on the underarm and along one side of the shirt. "As we were looking at that it became evident that this cut was done when the shirt was taken from the frozen body of someone who had been killed," says Thompson. "It fits a type and style that would be appropriate for the time period and some of the painted designs would be consistent with what would have been on Ghost Dance shirts."

Thompson says museum records show the shirt came from a "somewhat mysterious donor" who gave many Native American objects to the museum prior to 1925, along with a set of photographs taken on the Wounded Knee field and sold as souvenirs. "He was a prolific collector, yet there is no correspondence in the curator's papers dealing with these donations," says Thompson. And while Thompson says several researchers from the Cheyenne River Sioux have seen the shirt and would agree that it was likely taken at Wounded Knee, "an extra authentication would be desirable."

While no claim has been made for the shirt to be repatriated under NAGPRA, the museum now treats it as an important cultural object that must be handled in a very sensitive manner. "It was last on display more than twenty-five years ago in our old facility along with many other Native American objects that were not really well identified," says Thompson. "Now we would only display the shirt if we could provide adequate context and if we prepared the exhibit in consultation with people who may be descendants of the individual who might have been wearing that shirt and could help tell the story."

For now the museum keeps the shirt stored away. "It's shared cultural property the museum is holding in trust," says Thompson. "It has an important association to a really horrific event in American history and speaks very much to the power of objects."

State of Iowa Historical Museum
600 E. Locust
Des Moines, IA 50319
(515) 281-5111
www.iowahistory.org

IN COLD BLOOD TOMBSTONES AND GALLOWS

Kansas Museum of History (Topeka)

Visiting the graves of notorious killers and viewing artifacts connected to their crimes is a popular, if gruesome, pastime for many tourists. And while some towns and museums cash in on these connections, there's a long-running debate in Kansas over whether to display objects relating to the murderers of four members of the Clutter family, in Holcomb in 1959.

The grisly crime and its aftermath became the subject of Truman Capote's 1966 best-selling true-crime novel *In Cold Blood.* And in April 1965, when convicted murderers Richard Hickock and Perry Smith were hanged for their crimes, Capote paid for tombstones to be placed on their graves in the Mount Muncie Cemetery near the Lansing State Penitentiary.

If you go to that cemetery today, you'll see low granite headstones set in cement on Hickock's and Smith's graves. But those are not the stones Capote originally ordered and paid for. Those original headstones were stolen in 1980 and were then quietly replaced by the cemetery, which tried to avoid publicity by not reporting the theft to authorities.

The headstones of the *In Cold Blood* murderers were stolen and spent some time as the steps to a shed before ending up at the Kansas Historical Society. KANSAS STATE HISTORICAL SOCIETY

But the Kansas Bureau of Investigation, the agency that originally cracked the Clutter case, took note, and in December 2000 a KBI agent retrieved the stolen markers from a farm in Iola, Kansas. A friend of the man who had originally taken the markers from the cemetery was using them as steps to a shed.

While stolen property usually gets returned to its owners, this property had never been reported missing. Yet it was a judge who ended up deciding that because the cemetery would not put the stones back on the graves, the markers should instead go to the Kansas Historical Society in Topeka, for safekeeping.

Although those who were still mourning the Clutters objected, the historical society put the tombstones on display in the "What's New" section of the Kansas Museum of History, where people lined up to see them.

The markers were later put in storage, along with the trapdoor and other pieces of the gallows used to hang Hickock, Smith, and other Kansas criminals. For years the public could see images of the tombstones and the gallows on the museum website. But Blair Tarr, museum curator for the Kansas State Historical Society, says even those images were taken down around the fiftieth anniversary of the Clutter murders out of respect for the surviving family members and their relatives.

"There are a lot of people who feel strongly about this," says Tarr. "And any time the issue of capital punishment comes up in Kansas people talk about the Clutter murders and ask about the tombstones and the gallows." He says the museum staff has talked often about putting those objects on display, but might have to wait until the generation of the survivors passes. "I don't think anyone has a problem with us having and maintaining them," says Tarr, "but we need to find a responsible way to display them because they do generate so much controversy. We will eventually put together an exhibit that includes these items, informs the public about these issues, and encourages people to make up their own minds about right and wrong and crime and punishment. It may just have to wait awhile longer."

Kansas Museum of History
6425 SW 6th Ave.
Topeka, KS 66615
(785) 272-8681
www.kshs.org/museum

CREEPY THINGS AND LIVE AMMUNITION

Thomas D. Clark Center for Kentucky History (Frankfort)

Daniel Boone's death mask, Abraham Lincoln's pocket watch, a signature etched in glass by outlaw Jesse James, and a boxing robe that belonged to Kentucky-born Muhammad Ali are among the more than two thousand artifacts used to tell the story of Kentucky in the core exhibition at the Thomas D. Clark Center for Kentucky History in Frankfort.

But Trevor Jones, director of museum collections and exhibitions for the Kentucky Historical Society, says there are some objects that are considered too creepy, too odd, too disgusting, or just plain dangerous.

Live bullets removed from weapons are kept in a special ammunitions freezer.
COURTESY OF THE KENTUCKY HISTORICAL SOCIETY

A doll named "Jimmy" stays in storage because he "just scares the heck out of the museum team," says Jones. Indeed, with his pale, glassy eyes that never close, well-worn ivory complexion, and disintegrating shoes, Jimmy does somewhat resemble a corpse. On several occasions staff members have reported that Jimmy has moved, apparently on his own, to different places or positions in his storage cabinet or in the workroom. And now when things go wrong at the museum, Jimmy gets the blame.

Intact clothing found on the skeleton of a man dug up by the Kentucky Archaeological Survey was given to the Kentucky Historical Society before the skeleton was reburied. The clothes help tell the story of what people were wearing and getting buried in during the 1840s and '50s and Jones would someday like to display the well-preserved outfit in the museum. However, he says curators there think the clothing is too disgusting. "One curator didn't even want to be involved with the cataloging of the clothing," says Jones.

"Jimmy" stays in storage because he "just scares the heck out of the museum team."
KENTUCKY HISTORICAL SOCIETY

A beaded necklace known as the "cursed necklace" was dropped off anonymously at the museum along with a newspaper clipping from 1900 that details the curse. The clipping, which appeared in a Chicago newspaper, explains that in the 1820s a jilted girl from Kentucky made a cursed charm for her former lover that was designed to bring a string of misfortunes to his family every thirteen years. "We had an exhibit wall fall down the one time we displayed the necklace," says Jones, who notes that the next time the curse is scheduled to strike will be 2016.

And then there are the live bullets and bags of black powder removed from guns, rifles, cannonballs, and other weapons in the collection. "Those items are part of the artifacts," says Jones, "but we're not going to exhibit that material with the artifacts because it's just too dangerous." Instead, he says, the museum keeps that material in a special "ammunitions freezer" that's off-limits to employee lunches.

Jones says all the guns at the Kentucky Historical Society are unloaded and all the cannonballs inert, but he knows some smaller museums have discovered live shells and ammunition in objects that have been on display for many years. "They might have grenades they don't know are live. And there are a lot of things that look like cannonballs from the Civil War that are actually shells with powder in there," he says.

Kentucky Historical Society
Thomas D. Clark Center for Kentucky History
100 W. Broadway
Frankfort, KY 40601
(502) 564-1792
www.history.ky.gov

SPIRO T. AGNEW COLLECTION

Hornbake Library at the University of Maryland
(College Park)

When John Adams became the country's first vice president, he called the job "the most insignificant office that ever the invention of man contrived or his imagination conceived."

Ouch!

The job profile and responsibilities have changed a bit over the years, but US vice presidents still don't receive much attention. Nor do their papers and memorabilia once they leave office and once those materials make their way to libraries, museums, and other institutions for safekeeping. But, as with the collections of material related to US presidents, truly offbeat and intriguing objects often are mixed in with the papers.

Case in point: the Spiro T. Agnew Papers at the Hornbake Library at the University of Maryland in College Park.

Agnew served as Richard Nixon's vice president from January 20, 1969, until his resignation on October 10, 1973. Before that, the former vice president served as Baltimore County executive and governor of Maryland, which is presumably why the bulk of his papers and memorabilia ended up here.

The collection includes correspondence, campaign materials, briefing books, photographs, audio tapes, and memorabilia. And "in this case," says Elizabeth Novara, the library's curator of historical manuscripts, "there are hundreds of objects and artwork associated with the papers, including many gifts given to him from constituents and heads of states when he was vice president."

Novara says the objects from the collection rarely go on view mostly because the library has no permanent exhibit space and mounts just one temporary exhibit from its holdings each academic year. But not likely to ever go on exhibit is the monkey cape the president of Kenya gave to Agnew.

"It's animal skin and definitely has an 'interesting' smell," says Novara. "And a conservationist we asked to examine the cape suspected it was treated with DDT or some other chemicals to preserve it." No one knows what those chemicals were, "so we don't touch it. We don't put it on. It just stays in the box," she says, as does a zebra skin that was also found in the collection.

Vice President Spiro Agnew had his portrait painted many times. But this is probably the only image of Agnew rendered in feathers. SPIRO AGNEW PAPERS, SPECIAL COLLECTIONS, UNIVERSITY OF MARYLAND LIBRARIES

President Richard Nixon misspelled his own second-in-command's name when he wrote this thank-you note to "Spyro Agnew." SPIRO AGNEW PAPERS, SPECIAL COLLECTIONS, UNIVERSITY OF MARYLAND LIBRARIES

Many far less dangerous but still quite unusual objects stay tucked away as well.

Among the many portraits of Agnew is one the staff refers to as "Agnew with beaver teeth," one that portrays the former vice president as a clown with white face paint and a red nose, and another that is made out of feathers. "It was a gift from the president of the Republic of Indonesia that at first looks like a traditional painting. But get closer and you realize it's made entirely of different-colored bird feathers," says Novara.

And then there's the framed photograph of Agnew's one-time boss, former president Richard Nixon. The photograph bears a personalized, handwritten message from the president to his vice president, thanking him for his service to the nation. Unfortunately, the president misspelled Spiro Agnew's first name.

Proof, perhaps, that like the public, even some presidents don't pay much attention to the vice presidents.

Spiro T. Agnew Papers
Hornbake Library North
University of Maryland—College Park
College Park, MD 20734
(301) 405-9212
www.lib.umd.edu/hornbake

MASONIC URNS

Grand Lodge (Boston, Massachusetts)

Freemasonry has been around since at least the seventeenth century and today is mostly known as a private fraternity that does charitable deeds and works to build the values of its membership and make "good men better." It's also known as a society with secrets (but not a "secret society," Freemasons are quick to tell you) and an association of lodges men must ask to join and that uses symbols and rituals to bond its members together.

George Washington, Ben Franklin, James Garfield, and many other notable American figures from history were Masons. And throughout the 1800s and into the early to mid-1900s Freemasonry and similar fraternal organizations were extremely popular, with over six million people reportedly belonging to American fraternal groups in 1900.

Today the story of American Freemasonry and fraternalism is documented and shared at the Scottish Rite Masonic Museum & Library in historic Lexington, Massachusetts (formerly the National Heritage Museum). The museum presents exhibitions on a variety of topics in American history and popular culture and has a permanent collection with more than seventeen thousand artifacts.

Museum exhibits in Lexington have featured everything from Masonic quilts, textiles, art, and banners to photographs and decorative arts, as well as many non-Masonic, general history programs. But in the imposing granite building on the Boston Common that serves as the headquarters of the Grand Masonic Lodge of Massachusetts, which was organized in 1733 and is the oldest Grand Lodge in the Western Hemisphere, there are some historically significant ceremonial objects that most Freemasons don't even get to see.

For many years there was a small museum in the building where Masons and non-Masons could view artifacts from Masonic history, such as a Masonic apron worn by the Marquis de Lafayette, a photo of General Tom Thumb in his Masonic regalia, and a chair once owned by Henry Price, who is known as the father of Freemasonry in America. The museum was closed during a building renovation and these and many of the organization's other treasured objects are now on extended loan at the Scottish Rite Masonic Museum & Library in Lexington.

But for many history buffs, the real treasures owned by the Grand Lodge are several bunches of carved wooden grapes and two small gold urns.

Early Freemasons such as Paul Revere, John Hancock, and George Washington gathered at Boston's Bunch of Grapes Tavern to discuss politics and to plan action. The tavern opened in 1712 on King Street (now State Street) and was where Henry Price established the first lodge of Freemasons in America on July 30, 1733. Sketches made of the outside of the tavern at the time show three bunches of carved wooden grapes hanging in a triangular pattern outside the entrance. The grapes signaled to passersby that refreshments were available inside, in much the way a flashing neon BAR sign would do today.

Today a bunch of grapes hangs in the lobby of Corinthian Hall inside the Grand Lodge and is a replica carved with wood taken from the USS *Constitution* during its renovation and restoration in 1927. The only two remaining original bunches of grapes from the tavern are also at the Grand Lodge

Urns containing hair clipped from Presidents George Washington and James Garfield are used in special ceremonies by the Grand Lodge of Masons in Boston, Massachusetts. COLLECTION OF THE GRAND LODGE OF MASONS IN MASSACHUSETTS, PHOTOGRAPH BY DAVID BOHL

and in the possession of the St. John's Lodge, which meets at the Grand Lodge building. Those gold-painted wooden grapes are considered to be "witnesses" to important events in colonial and revolutionary Boston, and in Freemason history, and so the lodge keeps them locked away in a metal case and brings them out only during the installation ceremony of the new master of St. John's Lodge.

While the wooden grapes have been transformed from a mere tavern sign into a sacred relic, some other objects dear to the Masons have been symbolic from the start. The most historically significant object in the Grand Lodge collection is a gold urn that Paul Revere made not long after fellow Mason George Washington died in 1799. The urn is shaped like, and not much larger than, a fancy saltshaker and contains the lock of hair that Revere had asked Martha Washington to clip from her deceased husband's head.

Like the bunch of grapes, the urn, along with a similar one (not made by Revere) that holds a lock of hair snipped from the head of Freemason and US President James Garfield shortly after his death in September 1881 is kept locked in a vault at Boston's Grand Lodge.

Both urns are used in Grand Lodge ceremonies. The urn containing George Washington's hair leaves the vault only once every three years, when the Grand Lodge installs a new grand master. The urn containing the lock of hair from Garfield is carried in the procession when the grand master is installed for his second and third one-year terms.

The wooden grapes and the Revere urn have occasionally been put on display as part of special exhibitions, but Jeffrey Gardiner, grand secretary of the Grand Lodge of Masons in Massachusetts, says that although the items have historic significance beyond the Freemason society, for the most part, "we prefer to keep these treasures for the pleasure of the fraternity."

Scottish Rite Masonic Museum & Library
33 Marrett Rd.
Lexington, MA 02421
(781) 861-6559
www.nationalheritagemuseum.org

Sources include: Aimee E. Newell, Hilary Anderson Stelling, and Catherine Compton Swanson, *Curiosities of the Craft: Treasures from the Grand Lodge of Massachusetts Collection,* Boston: Grand Lodge of Masons in Massachusetts and the Scottish Rite Masonic Museum & Library, May 2013.

LIFELIKE GLASS SEA LIFE
AND HISTORICALLY SIGNIFICANT
INSECTS

Harvard's Museums (Cambridge, Massachusetts)

The Harvard Museum of Natural History in Cambridge, Massachusetts, is the public face of Harvard University's three major museums—the Museum of Comparative Zoology, the Harvard University Herbaria, and Harvard's Mineralogical and Geological Museum—and is filled with permanent and changing exhibits that draw from collections that together have more than twenty-one million specimens, many of which date back to the 1700s. Permanent exhibits include everything from microscopic mites and spiders to hummingbirds, reptiles, fish, and even dinosaurs.

In the historic, two-story Great Mammal Hall, which looks much as it did when it was first built in 1872, specimens include a full-size giraffe, a bison, a narwhal, and three whale skeletons, which are suspended from the ceiling. There are also some creatures on display that have become extinct, such as the Tasmanian tiger and the Steller's sea cow.

While these exhibits are quite popular, the Harvard Museum of Natural History is perhaps best known for the exhibit of 3,200 hand-crafted, life-size, and incredibly realistic glass models of flowering plants made between 1887 and 1936 by the father-and-son team of Leopold and Rudolph Blaschka.

The plants, which the Blaschkas made exclusively for Harvard, have had a dedicated gallery space since 1893, but no historic gallery space remains in the public museum to display the full collection of 433 exquisite, recently restored, and equally realistic Blaschka-made glass models of marine and terrestrial invertebrates that depict everything from jellyfish ("jellies"), sea anemones, and octopus to sea cucumbers, marine worms, and land snails. "As we are a science rather than an art museum, selected marine models are displayed only when they fit with our many changing natural history exhibitions," says Janis Sacco, director of exhibitions.

Among the Harvard museums' collections of more than twenty-nine million (non-glass) specimens are hundreds of thousands of type specimens,

Visitors love the exhibit of 3,200 realistic glass models of flowering plants at the Harvard Museum of Natural History, but no historic gallery space remains for this glass jellyfish and more than four hundred other glass creatures. MUSEUM OF COMPARATIVE ZOOLOGY, HARVARD UNIVERSITY. ALL ORIGINAL PHOTOGRAPHY IS © PRESIDENT AND FELLOWS OF HARVARD COLLEGE (MCZ SC-132)

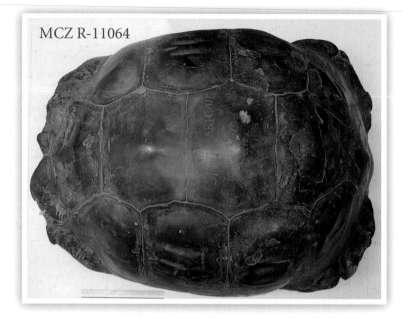

MCZ R-11064

Due to its scientific significance, this type specimen from an extinct species of giant Galapagos tortoise remains tucked away in the research collections at Harvard's Museum of Comparative Zoology. MUSEUM OF COMPARATIVE ZOOLOGY, HARVARD UNIVERSITY. ALL ORIGINAL PHOTOGRAPHY IS © PRESIDENT AND FELLOWS OF HARVARD COLLEGE (MCZ R-11064)

which are the original specimens used to describe a species or subspecies. Valuable and irreplaceable, "as a general policy, type specimens are not usually placed on exhibit due to their scientific significance, unless unusual circumstances warrant it," says Linda S. Ford, director of collections operations at Harvard's Museum of Comparative Zoology. That's why the type specimen from an extinct species of giant Galapagos tortoise from Floreana Island with an inscription carved into its shell by sailors from a whaling ship out of New Bedford, Massachusetts, the USS *Abigail*, remains in the research collections.

Logbooks indicate the USS *Abigail* sailed the Pacific Ocean under Captain Benjamin J. Clark from 1829 to 1835. And "thousands of these animals were loaded onto whaling ships to serve as a source of meat during long transoceanic voyages," says Jose Rosado, curatorial associate of herpetology. "They could survive for close to a year without food and water, so the tortoises could easily be stored in ships' holds till needed."

Perhaps that is part of the reason this species went extinct from Floreana between 1840 and 1850.

In addition to the scientifically important type specimens in Harvard's collections, there are some scientifically unremarkable specimens with intriguing historic connections. These include the Birdwing butterflies from Papua New Guinea that are all that's left of an expedition led by a scientist who was eaten by cannibals. And among the world's largest collection of ants is an ant that Stefan Cover, curatorial assistant in entomology, calls the "Stalin ant." This ant was collected on June 30, 1945, by Harvard professor Harlow Shapley, an astronomer also known for his studies of ants. While attending a banquet hosted by Soviet dictator Joseph Stalin for visiting US scientists, Shapley, the story goes, noticed an ant running across the table. Being a collector, he happened to have a glass vial in his pocket, so he filled it with vodka and took the ant home as both a souvenir of the dinner and as a specimen for Harvard.

And then there's the "surrender centipede."

While he was doing research on some of the museum's vast collection of centipedes, one specimen jar caught the eye of Rowland Shelley, curator of terrestrial invertebrates at the North Carolina State Museum of Natural Sciences in Raleigh. He noticed one vial was marked APPOMATTOX COURTHOUSE, APRIL 9, 1865, which Shelley knew was the day General Robert E. Lee surrendered to General Ulysses S. Grant at the end of the Civil War.

The collector's name wasn't listed, but Shelley figured out that the naturalist Theodore Lyman was among the Union soldiers at the surrender site. "Lee got there first, and Grant was late," says Shelley. "So I can envision Theodore Lyman getting there at the appointed time, or maybe a little bit early, and kicking over some logs or something while he waited and finding this centipede."

It is a common Virginia species, but Shelley believes its link with history sets it apart and hopes that the "surrender centipede" will eventually be displayed in a place of honor.

Harvard Museum of Natural History
26 Oxford St.
Cambridge, MA 02138
(617) 495-3045
www.hmnh.harvard.edu

DRUNKEN MONKEYS DIORAMA AND FORD MODEL T VIOLIN

The Henry Ford (Dearborn, Michigan)

Henry Ford was not only the founder of the Ford Motor Company, he was a big fan of the assembly line as a tool for mass production and an inventor with more than 160 patents in his name. Ford was also one of the richest men in the world, and happily spent a large chunk of his fortune collecting objects for a museum to celebrate industrial history and to "give people a true picture of the development of the country."

To that end, in the late 1920s Ford built a single-story, nine-acre exhibit hall in Dearborn, Michigan, that was not far from his Rouge Plant, which was then the world's largest industrial complex. Ford named the museum the Edison Institute in honor of his friend and mentor, Thomas Edison, and in 1933 the facility popularly known now as The Henry Ford opened its doors to the public. (The destination now includes five attractions: The Henry Ford Museum, Greenfield Village, an IMAX theater, the Ford Rouge Factory Tour, and a research center.)

Billed, then and now, as one of the most important collections of Americana in the United States, the Henry Ford appears to have room in the museum to display just about everything in its collection, from bicycles, buses, stagecoaches, and of course, automobiles, to airplanes and giant locomotives.

Iconic artifacts on display include George Washington's camp chest and bed, the oldest surviving steam engine in the world, and the bus in which Rosa Parks was riding when she made her historic stand for civil rights in December 1955. The museum also displays the world's most accurate reproduction of the 1903 Wright Flyer, the plane Orville and Wilbur Wright built in their Dayton, Ohio, bicycle shop and flew at Kill Devil Hills, North Carolina, on December 17, 1903, when they completed the first heavier-than-air, machine-powered flight in the world. (The Wright family home and the cycle shop where Wilbur and Orville worked on the Wright Flyer are among the buildings in Greenfield Village, an eighty-acre village adjacent to the Henry Ford Museum that is dotted with eighty-three authentic historic structures, including the Illinois courthouse where Abraham Lincoln practiced law and the house Noah Webster lived in while working on the first American dictionary.)

Other exhibits in the Henry Ford Museum include inventions; appliances; the only existing example of R. Buckminster Fuller's efficient, domed Dymaxion House; and some odd treasures of American history, such as the rocking chair President Abraham Lincoln was sitting in at Ford's Theatre when he was assassinated on April 14, 1865; the limousine President John F. Kennedy was riding in when he was assassinated on November 22, 1963, in Dallas, Texas; and a test tube sealed and taken from the bedroom where Thomas Edison took his last breath.

As big as it is, the Henry Ford still has plenty of treasures tucked away. Among those are some offbeat-but-heartfelt gifts given to Henry Ford for which curators just can't seem to find a place out on the floor.

One is a diorama made out of peach pits, wood, paper, tin, lead, and glass showing monkeys gambling, drinking, and working in a saloon—all activities that the diorama maker, Massachusetts State Prison inmate Patrick Culhane,

This diorama of about seventy monkeys gambling, drinking, and working in a saloon was made by a prisoner at the Massachusetts State Prison in Boston and presented to Henry Ford. FROM THE COLLECTIONS OF THE HENRY FORD. (15.1.1/ THF49082)

believed led otherwise upstanding people astray. Culhane's artwork was presented to Henry Ford in 1914 and Ford later arranged for Culhane to get a job in a Ford Motor Company plant when he was released from prison. That wasn't so unusual—Ford was known for advocating a liberal employment policy in his plants to give people who might be discriminated against elsewhere a chance. That included people with physical and mental disabilities and ex-convicts who, according to museum records, were often released on parole through special arrangements between the company and penitentiary officials.

Other treasures curators keep in storage include some of the more than six hundred musical instruments in a collection that spans the seventeenth to twentieth centuries and includes spinets, fifes, drums, clarinets, pianos, harps, and many other stringed, brass, and woodwind instruments, both mass-produced

In 1932 a farmer from Alabama made this full-size standard tenor violin using parts from a discarded 1923 Ford Model T touring car.
FROM THE COLLECTIONS OF THE HENRY FORD.
(32.665.1/THF153054)

and handmade. The collection includes some seventeenth- and eighteenth-century violins Henry Ford purchased in the 1920s that were made by master violinmakers Antonio Stradivari and Giuseppe Guarneri del Gesu, and an unusual one given to Ford by an Alabama farmer named Clay Speegle.

Speegle apparently had some spare time on his hands in 1932 and spent about thirty days making a full-size, standard tenor violin out of parts taken from a discarded 1923 Ford Model T touring car.

Museum records describing the violin don't say whether the instrument was playable when it arrived, but they do note which parts of the Model T Speegle used. For example, the violin body, which is painted brown, is made from the dust shield, the metal that joins the running board to the body of the car. Wood framing from the car's body was used to make the sound post, the neck, the scroll, the finger board, and some other parts of the instrument.

Not only did Speegle have the time and skill to make the violin, he was moved to write a poem about it, from the car's point of view. Titled "The Past and Present History of the Violin," it reads in part:

When I got old and worn and shackley,

Though I had done a might lot,

They cast me in the junk pile,

To lie there rust and rot.

But some parts of me was selected

The parts that best would do

And now I am put together

With solder and with glue.

The full poem, printed in a local newspaper at the time, remains tucked away at the Henry Ford Museum, along with the Model T violin.

The Henry Ford
20900 Oakwood Blvd.
Dearborn, MI 48124
(313) 982-6001 or (800) 835-5237
www.thehenryford.org

Sources include: Object reports from the collections of The Henry Ford.

INVISIBLE ART

Walker Art Center (Minneapolis, Minnesota)

There are more than eleven thousand works of modern and contemporary art in the permanent collection of the Walker Art Center in Minneapolis, Minnesota, and the galleries of this major art museum are filled with a tantalizing array of paintings, sculptures, film/video, photography, and other works in a wide variety of other traditional and new media.

Seeded with the eclectic collection lumber magnate Thomas Barlow Walker began in the mid-1870s, the Walker honed in on contemporary art in the 1940s, acquiring works by artists such as Pablo Picasso, Henry Moore, Edward Hopper, and Georgia O'Keeffe. In the 1960s, work by Andy Warhol, Chuck Close, George Segal, Donald Judd, Claes Oldenburg, and their contemporaries joined the collection and now the treasures held at the Walker and the range of artists celebrated by the museum are almost too numerous to list.

Today every performance piece, installation, and work of art (including the quirky first Internet Cat Video Festival, held in 2012) is carefully chosen to meet the museum's stated goal of being "a catalyst for the creative expression of artists and the active engagement of audiences." But visitors might find it especially challenging to engage with *Anonymous II,* a work by Belgian artist Kris Martin that Walker Art Center curator Betsy Carpenter described as the center's "only invisible artwork."

While the piece is not locked away in a cabinet, the work is almost impossible to find.

It consists of an anonymous human skeleton that was buried on the museum grounds on April 20, 2009, as part of an exhibition titled *The Quick and the Dead* that included artwork that dealt with the passage of time. A certificate signed by the artist and displayed in a gallery in the museum gives the GPS coordinates of the skeleton's burial site, but because the site itself is unmarked beneath an open green space, the artwork will remain hidden forever and can only be imagined by the viewer.

"Reduced to a mere specimen for medical study, this set of bones is restored to some degree of personhood through his internment, though its identity remains unknown," wrote then–Walker curator Peter Eleey when the piece was first installed. "In both this anonymity and the uncertainty of its location, the skeleton assumes a vast but invisible presence, becoming a metonymic figure for death itself."

While the idea of an "invisible" work of art may seem sort of strange, Carpenter says it wasn't a big stretch for the museum or for the artist. "There's a long legacy in the Conceptual Art movement of the idea being paramount to the object," says Carpenter, who explains that removing something from view by burying it—temporarily or forever—has been one of the ways many artists have expressed and embraced the idea. "Kris Martin has expanded upon the strategies of conceptual artists of the 1960s and '70s. His practice delves into the most profound philosophical and existential human issues of life and

In *Anonymous II* artist Kris Martin had an unidentified human skeleton buried in an unmarked location on the Walker Art Museum grounds. COLLECTION WALKER ART CENTER, MINNEAPOLIS; T. B. WALKER ACQUISITION FUND, 2008. PHOTOGRAPH COURTESY WALKER ART CENTER. SKELETON GIFT TO KIKI SMITH FROM DAVID WOJNAROWICZ, GIFTED TO THE WALKER ART CENTER. COURTESY SIES + HÖKE, DÜSSELDORF. PHOTOGRAPHER GENE PITTMAN, MINNEAPOLIS

death, time and absence through his recontextualization of found objects that have their own symbolic import and histories—in this instance, a human skeleton originally used for medical study. By returning the anonymous skeleton to the earth in an unmarked grave and providing only the longitudinal and latitudinal coordinates to the museum visitor, Martin makes a simple and yet grand gesture toward the tradition of the memento mori, which reminds us that our time here is fleeting, and death awaits us all," she says. "It's the most modest artwork you can imagine."

While the skeleton in *Anonymous II* is anonymous and was once used as a medical specimen, it does have an interesting connection to the art world that adds an extra layer of meaning to the work. When the *Anonymous II* installation was purchased, it was the museum's responsibility to obtain the skeleton to be buried. "We were looking at medical skeletons," says Carpenter, "but then one of our curators remembered that Kiki Smith, an artist we'd done an exhibition with awhile back, had a skeleton in her studio that another noted artist, David Wojnarowicz, had given her a few years before his death. Smith gave us the skeleton to use in the Kris Martin piece."

When *Anonymous II* is "exhibited" at the Walker, all the visitor encounters in the gallery is the certificate that includes the GPS coordinates. "The buried skeleton is the artwork," says Carpenter. "The certificate of authenticity is not art but was provided by the artist and his gallery and is common practice with works of a more conceptual nature. The artist supported our idea of exhibiting the certificate as a way for our audience to know that the work is installed underground, 'on view' as it were. But there is no mandate for us to show the certificate."

Walker Art Center
1750 Hennepin Ave.
Minneapolis, MN 55403
(612) 375-7600
www.walkerart.org

Sources include: Peter Eeley, "Kris Martin, *Anonymous II,*" *Art on Call,* November 19, 2009; Peter Eeley, Olaf Blanke, Ina Blom, Peter Osborne, and Margaret and Christine Wertheim, *The Quick and the Dead,* p. 246, Walker Art Center, 2009.

TRUMAN'S PORTRAIT ON THE HEAD OF A PIN

Harry S. Truman Library and Museum
(Independence, Missouri)

The Harry S. Truman Library and Museum opened on July 6, 1957, and sits on a hill overlooking Truman's boyhood home of Independence, Missouri. Exhibits tell the story of Truman's presidency and personal life with interactive audio and video elements and displays that draw on a collection of thirty thousand objects. Included in those holdings are gifts to President and Mrs. Truman from private citizens and foreign heads of state, political cartoons, personal possessions of the Truman family, a collection of Abraham Lincoln memorabilia, and a wide range of political memorabilia and objects associated with Truman's career, particularly with his presidency. Some of the special objects in the collection include a safety plug pulled from the atomic bomb dropped on Nagasaki, flags from the Kon-Tiki craft sailed by explorer Thor Heyerdahl, and the original THE BUCK STOPS HERE sign that sat on Truman's Oval Office desk.

The country's thirty-third commander in chief helped design the library and museum building and spent most days working at his desk in his office there after his term as president, which lasted from 1945 until January 1953. The museum staff would often find the president already at work when they arrived for duty and there are numerous stories of Truman answering the library phone, dealing with callers' questions, and giving directions to visitors who were no doubt surprised to learn that they were actually speaking with the former president.

After Truman passed away in 1972, his office became one of the museum's more popular exhibits. But while papers and other materials were removed from most of the drawers in Truman's desk and credenza shortly after his death, it wasn't until 1993 that two drawers in the credenza behind the desk were unlocked.

"Apparently the staff member or members who originally removed the papers from Truman's office hadn't been able to open those drawers. And as staff changed over the years, no one remembered that the drawers had never been opened," says museum curator Clay Bauske. Years later, one curious staff member decided to find out once and for all what was in those drawers and rummaged through a box of unidentified old keys until she found one that fit the locks.

Inside the drawers were souvenir cufflinks, lapel pins, miscellaneous documents, and assorted mementos. "There was no particular rhyme or reason for what was in there," says Bauske. "Even some of his canceled checks from the first decade of the twentieth century were there." Evidently the president was like a lot of us: When unsure about what to do with something, he put it in a junk drawer rather than throw it away.

"He apparently used the drawers as a convenient place to put things that had accumulated on his desk," says Bauske, "although his desktop was never tidy. He tended to work around the clutter."

For years museum staff at the Harry S. Truman Library and Museum were unable to unlock a drawer in the credenza in President Truman's office. When they did, they found an image of the president's face etched into the head of a pin. PHOTOGRAPH BY PHIL LICATA, COURTESY OF HARRY S. TRUMAN LIBRARY, INDEPENDENCE, MISSOURI

The drawer also contained one special, very tiny hidden treasure: a portrait of Truman on the head of a pin. The name of the artist who painted the portrait and the circumstances under which it was given to Truman are still unknown, but the red-velvet-lined silver case holding an inch-long glass tube was found intact.

"When we originally found this item in the locked drawer, we thought it was a fuse," says Bauske. "We cataloged and kept virtually everything Truman had in his office, whether significant or not, and it was only upon further inspection that we realized one end of the tube was a small magnifying glass that enlarged the image on the pin."

Since then the museum has occasionally displayed the tiny portrait, and when it does, provides a magnifying glass to allow visitors to see the detail.

There's another treasure the museum could not display for a long time because it was thought to be "lost" and turned out to be hidden in the president's attic.

In a White House ceremony in 1946, President Truman was presented with a valuable nine-hundred–year–old vase by a delegation from South Korea. During the 1970s and 1980s the museum was contacted numerous times about the location of that vase, but it could not be found anywhere in the museum storage areas, and museum staff had no luck tracking it down at other institutions, such as the Smithsonian.

"Then, in the mid-1980s, following the death of Bess Truman and the settlement of her will, we found among the materials a simple white box that had been stored in the attic of the Truman home," says Bauske. A note written in pencil on the box, in what Bauske says appears to be Bess Truman's writing, said simply "brown vase." The box did have a vase inside, but it was broken in several places. And it wasn't brown, but more of a gray-green color. "It was clearly the missing Korean vase," says Bauske.

No one can say for sure why Bess Truman described the vase as brown, how it got broken, or why it was hidden away, but once it was found, it was repaired and put on temporary display in the museum.

Harry S. Truman Library and Museum
500 W. US Hwy 24
Independence, MO 64050
(816) 268-8200
www.trumanlibrary.org

HUMAN-SKIN WALLETS

Museum of Osteopathic Medicine (Kirksville, Missouri)

The human body—and what heals it—can be a mystery, and there are many who believe that we shouldn't rely solely on traditional medical science for all the answers.

An early adopter of that premise was Andrew Taylor Still, who in the early nineteenth century was a traditionally trained Midwest doctor and surgeon treating patients with procedures such as bloodletting and blistering, which were among the standard practices of the day.

Heartbreaking personal tragedies and a stint as a Civil War doctor led Still to search for different methods of healing and he eventually developed his own set of theories and techniques based on the belief that diseases could be cured by such treatments as shaking, massaging, and otherwise manipulating the body.

Officially dubbing his new philosophy of medicine "osteopathy" in 1874, Still began teaching in 1892 at the American School of Osteopathy (now the A. T. Still University of Health Sciences) in Kirksville, Missouri. Today doctors of Osteopathic Medicine (DOs) are fully licensed physicians taught to blend more modern osteopathic beliefs with conventional medical procedures.

The life story of Andrew Taylor Still and the heritage and development of osteopathy are among the core stories told at the Museum of Osteopathic Medicine on the university's campus. Established in 1934 by Still's daughter, Blanche Still Laughlin, the museum is now housed in a glass-fronted building with a two-story atrium (Heritage Hall) that contains the small, two-room classroom building that housed Still's osteopathy school from 1892 to 1894 and his birthplace log cabin, which was moved from Virginia in 1929.

Both historic structures have photographs, artifacts, and audio installations that describe the family's frontier life and the school's early years. And three adjacent galleries are filled with a small portion of the fifty thousand objects, photographs, documents, and books dating from the early 1800s to the present that are in the museum's collection. Some exhibits explore the nineteenth-century medical practices—such as bloodletting, dosing, and blistering—for which osteopathy was created as an alternative, and include a display of the wide variety of early tools used in the profession. Other exhibits display surgical instruments, human bones, skulls, and a rare, fully dissected human nervous system created at the school in 1925—one of only four such dissections known to exist. (The school did another version in 1935–1936, which is now at the Smithsonian Institution in Washington, DC.)

Among the items the museum does not currently display are two wallets and a scrapbook made from what museum staff says is skin taken from human cadavers that were used in early anatomy classes at the school.

"Back then, cadavers weren't as respected as they are now," says museum curator Debra Loguda-Summers. "If anyone nowadays would do that, they'd get kicked out of school." Loguda-Summers says the scrapbook was purchased at an Iowa yard sale in 2010 and was created around 1916 by F. A. Gordon, a former student who filled the book with 244 images documenting student life in Kirksville. The scrapbook was brought to the museum because the donor thought the photos would have historical interest, but only upon close inspection was it discovered that the cover of the scrapbook had been made from the human cadaver skin of the chest, knee, and thigh.

This wallet, made from human skin, is part of the collection at the Museum of Osteopathic Medicine. MUSEUM OF OSTEOPATHIC MEDICINE^{SM}, KIRKSVILLE, MISSOURI [2004.77.47]

The wallets, hand stitched with white human skin on the outside and black human skin on the inside, were created by Frank Gasperich, who graduated from the osteopathy school around 1930. "Dr. Gasperich used one of the wallets on a regular basis and his name is embossed inside," says Loguda-Summers.

The wallets became part of the museum's collection in 2004 and were displayed briefly in 2006, when the museum unveiled a major exhibit tracing the history of Western anatomical study from ancient Greek medicine to the present. That exhibit includes anatomical illustrations, dissection-related artifacts, a full-size transparent anatomical mannequin, and details about the history of body-snatching, the old and ghoulish practice of digging up corpses from graveyards and selling the bodies to medical schools for dissection.

In 2006, Missouri residents were debating issues relating to embryonic stem cell research and Loguda-Summer says that at that time the president of the school asked the museum to put the human-skin wallets back in storage.

Museum of Osteopathic Medicine
A. T. Still University of Health Sciences
800 W. Jefferson St.
Kirksville, MO 63501
(660) 626-2359
www.atsu.edu/museum

RADIENDOCRINATOR

National Atomic Testing Museum (Las Vegas, Nevada)

Although it has the word "atomic" in its title and is devoted to documenting the science, technology, and history of nuclear weapons testing in Nevada and elsewhere, there's no need to wear lead-lined clothing when visiting the National Atomic Testing Museum in Las Vegas, Nevada.

"We do have some pieces of orange Fiesta dinnerware and dials painted with radium that are very slightly radioactive," says curator Karen Green, "but they won't harm you. They're here so people can use the Geiger counters we have on display and hear the clicking."

The rest of the museum's collection of more than twelve thousand artifacts includes photographs, videos, scientific instruments, nuclear reports, tools, and other objects that document the making of the first atomic bomb and the technology, scientific research, and planning that went into conducting nuclear testing above and below ground at the Nevada test site near Las Vegas and other places around the world.

In the museum, not only can visitors see artifacts related to nuclear testing technology, they can view a simulated bomb blast in Ground Zero Theater, watch footage of the more than one thousand nuclear bombs that were tested in the Nevada desert, and learn how citizens were once instructed to "duck and cover" to survive an atomic bomb blast.

On the popular culture side, there's a case filled with food, comic books, cookbooks, toys, games, memorabilia, and other commercial items with mushroom clouds and other nuclear-related imagery associated with the Atomic Age of the 1950s and '60s. There are also items on display that relate to the atomic tourism that took place in and around Las Vegas during the nuclear testing. "People would come to Las Vegas in order to see an atomic bomb go off," says Green. "There were atomic cocktail parties on roofs. There were special lookout spots where people would gather to see the mushroom clouds. And we have postcards, photographs, and other items related to that."

The museum also has a popular exhibit exploring the myths and realities of Area 51, the restricted area of Edwards Air Force Base in southern Nevada where stealth aircraft and atomic weapons were developed and tested and where some believe the government was secretly studying the aliens and alien spacecraft said to have landed near Roswell, New Mexico, in 1947. The exhibit includes everything from pieces of experimental planes to a UFO-hunting kit.

Most of the items donated to the museum are unclassified, but Green says there are some things she must be careful about putting on display because of the casual classification. "When I put something out, I have to think about if there's anything in the technology of the object that could put the technology being used today in jeopardy."

But that's not exactly what's keeping the museum from displaying the radiendocrinator.

Manufactured around 1930, the "radiendocrinator" male enhancement device contained strips of radium worn under the scrotum like a jock strap. FROM THE COLLECTION OF THE NATIONAL ATOMIC TESTING MUSEUM, LAS VEGAS, NEVADA

The gadget was donated to the museum by a man who walked in carrying a briefcase inside a lead-lined bag. "The radiendocrinator had belonged to his father and to his grandfather. He knew what it was and he knew it was radioactive, but he was moving and didn't know what to do with it, so he brought it to the museum," says Green.

She says that from the early 1900s into the 1940s and 1950s there were a wide variety of products marketed that contained some sort of radioactive material thought to be beneficial to health. "Some things were said to help memory. Others addressed goiters and fatigue. This particular object, which contained papers soaked in radium, was for sexual rejuvenation and was supposed to help you be a better man."

Green did a bit of research and learned that the device was invented by William J. A. Bailey around 1930 and sold back then as a "male enhancer" for the hefty price of $150. "It was to be placed in an athletic strap and worn under the scrotum at night to give the wearer control over life and bodily health," says Green. "It was also suggested that it be used in conjunction with drinking radium water."

Green says that after the radiendocrinator was donated to the museum, the staff tossed around suggestions on how to display it. "We may someday have a display of objects relating to radium and health effects, but for now we still have not come up with a tasteful way to display this object. We're working on it."

National Atomic Testing Museum
755 E. Flamingo Rd.
Las Vegas, NV 89119
(702) 794-5151
www.nationalatomictestingmuseum.org

HIDDEN CLUES IN A MUSIC BOX

Morris Museum (Morristown, New Jersey)

Housed in a Georgian-style mansion that has been added onto over time to accommodate a growing permanent collection of tantalizing objects, artifacts, and collections related to art, science, theater, and history, the Morris Museum in Morristown, New Jersey, is one of those "something for everyone" destinations.

That's why W. Anthony Sheppard and his family stopped by the museum in 2011 on a holiday-weekend road trip between Vermont and New Jersey.

Sheppard and his wife had visited the museum seventeen years earlier to see the art collection, but since then the museum had become home to the fabled Murtogh D. Guinness collection, which includes seven hundred historic mechanical musical instruments and automata (mechanical figures) as well as more than five thousand programmed media, ranging from player-piano rolls to pinned cylinders.

Guinness, a member of the prominent Anglo-Irish brewing family, had lived with his collection—which included everything from tiny music boxes to huge fairground organs—in twin, side-by-side New York City town houses. His will stipulated that the collection be kept together and enjoyed and not broken up and stored silently behind glass. The Morris Museum honors that request by displaying much of the collection in a special wing at the museum, presenting daily live demonstrations of several objects from the collection, and making audio and video clips of many of the instruments and automata in the collection available online and in the museum.

That's how Sheppard, a musicologist who teaches at Williams College in Massachusetts, came to discover a treasure hidden inside one of the music boxes on display. Sheppard says that while visiting the museum in 2011 he spent most of his time in the room of music boxes while his children ran ahead "to check out the self-playing banjo and the chair that emits tunes at each sitting." Snippets of tunes on a harmoniphone—a Swiss cylinder musical box with a reed organ, dating from 1877—caught his ear.

Four of the six tunes in the harmoniphone's repertoire were available for visitors to listen to, and these included tunes Puccini had used as sources

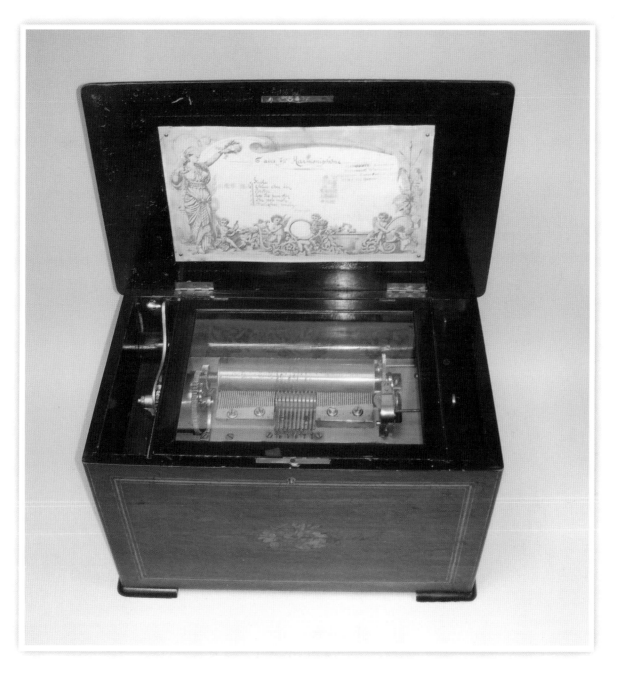

A serendipitous discovery at the Morris Museum may have revealed hidden secrets about the opera *Madame Butterfly*. The key? This music box. THE MURTOGH D. GUINNESS COLLECTION OF MECHANICAL MUSICAL INSTRUMENTS AND AUTOMATA, MORRIS MUSEUM, MORRISTOWN, NEW JERSEY, WWW.MORRISMUSEUM.ORG

for some musical themes in two of his well-known operas: *Turandot,* set in China, and *Madama Butterfly,* which is set in Japan.

"This box was made for the Chinese market with Chinese tunes," says Kelly McCartney, curator of the museum's Guinness Collection. "And Sheppard recognized specific musical arrangements and a tune in the box that is a major foundation and theme in *Madama Butterfly.* Previous to this, it was thought that the origins of the *Madama Butterfly* compositions were Japanese."

The tune wasn't the only clue that made Sheppard think that perhaps the history books on opera might need to be updated. "The tune sheet listing the melodies includes the titles in Chinese characters, allowing me to trace the origins of the melodies Puccini used. The tune sheet also includes the stamps of a Shanghai department store and a repair shop in Rome that operated in the early twentieth century, revealing the early journeys of this artifact," says Sheppard.

This box's six musical arrangements (shown on the tune program card in Chinese characters and English letters) suggest it was made for sale to China, a long-time consumer of European-made mechanical musical instruments and automata. THE MURTOGH D. GUINNESS COLLECTION OF MECHANICAL MUSICAL INSTRUMENTS AND AUTOMATA, MORRIS MUSEUM, MORRISTOWN, NEW JERSEY, WWW.MORRISMUSEUM.ORG

By studying the tunes and the box and tracing their history, Sheppard concluded that not only did Puccini use Chinese compositions for signature arrangements in *Madama Butterfly,* but the box in the Guinness collection is likely the very one that Puccini heard. "This particular object is an operatic Rosetta stone for Puccini's *Madama Butterfly* and *Turandot* and for understanding the global circulation of music in the late nineteenth century," says Sheppard.

He believes the clues were just waiting for someone who knew Puccini's operas and was interested in Chinese music.

And for someone who understood that a museum treasure can be hidden in plain sight.

Morris Museum
6 Normandy Heights Rd.
Morristown, NJ 07960
(973) 971-3700
www.morrismuseum.org

Sources include: W. Anthony Sheppard, "Music Box as Muse to Puccini's 'Butterfly,'" *New York Times,* June 15, 2012.

OUR LADY PHOTO

Museum of International Folk Art
(Santa Fe, New Mexico)

Opened in 1953, the Museum of International Folk Art (MOIFA) in Santa Fe, New Mexico, has more than 135,000 artifacts and is home to the world's largest collection of folk art.

The museum has a Hispanic Heritage Wing devoted to the art and heritage of Hispanic/Latino cultures and a whimsical and very popular long-term exhibition in its Girard Wing that showcases about ten thousand folk-art toys, miniatures, masks, costumes, and textiles from more than one hundred nations.

A wide variety of changing exhibitions are offered at MOIFA, and in February 2001 the museum presented one of the country's first computer art shows. *Cyber Arte: Tradition Meets Technology* featured the work of four Hispanic/Latina/Chicana artists who were exploring traditional elements by using technology, and was curated by Tey Marianna Nunn, then a curator at the museum and now the director of the Museum and Visual Arts Program at the National Hispanic Cultural Center in Albuquerque, New Mexico.

Nunn included five pieces by Mexican-born Alma López in the show, including *Our Lady,* a digital collage that portrays the popular religious and cultural Mexican icon the Virgen de Guadalupe (also known as Our Lady of Guadalupe) in a modern way.

Nunn felt the piece had "an important and timely message about Hispanic culture and especially about Hispanas and Latinas" and notes that many artists and leaders of religious and political movements, including César Chávez of the United Farm Workers, have referenced and reinterpreted the traditional image of the Virgen de Guadalupe in their work.

López grew up seeing the image "in churches, in the community, on tattoos, and on murals," and viewed the saint as "a strong, omnipresent female figure" in her life. So in 1998, when López received a grant to create digital prints using archival ink on specially treated canvas, one of the works she created was *Our Lady.* The piece is a small, 14-inch-by-17.5-inch image that depicts the saint as a real, contemporary woman wearing a modest two-piece resembling a swimsuit made from a garland of flowers.

López never imagined the piece would offend anyone or cause any debate, but shortly after the show opened at the museum, a firestorm of controversy erupted. Some called the artwork, dubbed the "Bikini Virgin," blasphemous, sacrilegious, and an "outrageous desecration." And Nunn, López, and the museum became the center of a swirling debate that touched on issues

A great deal of controversy erupted when the Museum of International Folk Art displayed *Our Lady* by Alma Lopez. MUSEUM OF INTERNATIONAL FOLK ART, IFAF COLLECTION. GIFT OF DR. FREDERICK M. NUNN AND SUSAN C. KARANT-NUNN. PHOTO BY: PAUL SMUTKO. *OUR LADY* BY ALMA LOPEZ, SANTA MONICA, CA © 1999 (SPECIAL THANKS TO RAQUEL SALINAS & RAQUEL GUTIERREZ) DIGITAL PRINT ON CANVAS (FA.2002.53.1)

relating to everything from First Amendment rights, censorship, sexuality, and class to who owned the Guadalupe image and controlled the right to its use.

During the show's run, busloads of protesters showed up outside the museum to denounce the work and hold prayer vigils, church leaders expressed their disapproval of the work, and death and bomb threats were made against the artist, the museum, and its staff. Public hearings were held, lawsuits were filed, and Nunn says the museum ended up writing a letter of apology to the Archbishop of Santa Fe and closing the exhibition early "in the spirit of conciliation."

Due in no small part to the controversy around the image and the role the image had in the museum's history, a collector purchased a digital print of *Our Lady* from López and donated it to the museum. But while the piece is now part of the permanent collection, it remains in storage. "We don't want to bring up that controversy in the community again," is the way one museum staff member explains it.

Tey Marianna Nunn, the curator who first chose to include *Our Lady* in the 2001 exhibition, understands the museum's decision not to display the work again. But because she considers the work "significant to American and Latino art history as well as to the institution where it made history," she hopes that it will someday be exhibited again for visitors to view, discuss, and debate.

For her part, López, who has put together a book about the controversy, is not surprised that the Museum of International Folk Art considers *Our Lady* a museum treasure it most likely will not exhibit again. "The response to this small print was violent beyond any of our imaginings," she says. And while in retrospect she believes the controversy was less about her work and more about larger issues ranging from "hatred of women's bodies and homophobia" to issues within the Catholic Archdiocese, López believes *Our Lady* "needs to be present, even if she's not seen."

Museum of International Folk Art
706 Camino Lejo
Santa Fe, NM 87504
(505) 476-1200
www.internationalfolkart.org

Sources include: Tey Marianna Nunn, "The Cyber Arte Exhibition: A Curator's Journey Through Community and Controversy," Smithsonian Center for Latino Initiatives: The Interpretation and Representation of Latino Cultures, Research and Museum Conference presentation, 2003.

GLASS COFFIN

Corning Museum of Glass (Corning, New York)

There's much more that can be made from glass than windows, windshields, and wine goblets.

And that becomes clear—as glass—after a tour through the Corning Museum of Glass, in Corning, New York. It is here that visitors learn about the incredibly far-reaching role of glass in art, history, culture, technology, science, craft, and design.

The museum was established in 1951 by Corning Glass Works (now Corning Incorporated) and its Glass Collection Galleries span thirty-five centuries and feature glass found in nature as well as man-made glasswork from

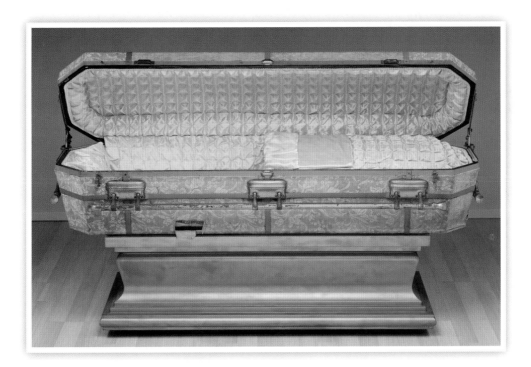

Very few of these six-hundred-pound glass caskets were ever sold, but one of them is in storage at the Corning Museum of Glass. 2001.4.234 COLLECTION OF THE CORNING MUSEUM OF GLASS, CORNING, NEW YORK, GIFT OF FRED HUNTER

ancient to modern times. Visitors can not only watch live glassmaking demonstrations, they can sign up on the spot for short (twenty- to forty-minute) classes in hot glassmaking, flameworking, fusing, and sandblasting.

For those who would rather just wander the galleries, there are displayed treasures ranging from a glass portrait of an ancient Egyptian pharaoh to

Doeskin embossed with leaves and flowers hid the fact that this coffin was made of glass. 2001.4.234 COLLECTION OF THE CORNING MUSEUM OF GLASS, CORNING, NEW YORK, GIFT OF FRED HUNTER

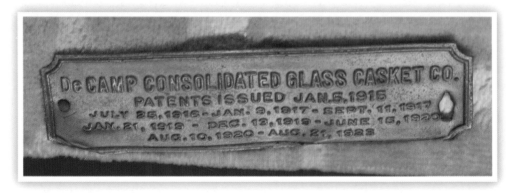

2001.4.234 COLLECTION OF THE CORNING MUSEUM OF GLASS, CORNING, NEW YORK, GIFT OF FRED HUNTER

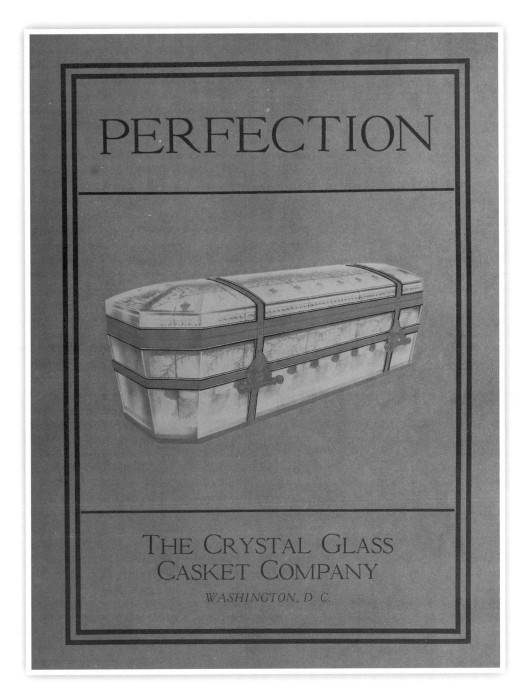

PERFECTION

THE CRYSTAL GLASS CASKET COMPANY

WASHINGTON, D. C.

"Most companies claiming to produce glass coffins turned out to be fronts to attract investors, and most investors saw no returns," says Tina Oldknow, the curator of modern glass at the Corning Museum of Glass. BIB #70545 COLLECTION OF THE RAKOW RESEARCH LIBRARY, THE CORNING MUSEUM OF GLASS

Venetian glass, Tiffany glass, a two-hundred–inch telescope mirror, and more than one thousand glass paperweights (one of the largest collections of its kind). There's also a tower made of more than one hundred Pyrex casserole dishes, a glass slipper made for a film version of *Cinderella* that was never completed, and a tiny, incredibly realistic-looking glass strawberry covered with that cottonlike fuzzy mold we sometimes encounter in store-bought containers of fruit. Curators occasionally bring out the glass bullets, a salesman's sample box of glass eyes, and the electric iron made of Pyrex that was developed during World War II in an effort to conserve metal, but the six-hundred–pound glass coffin stays high on a shelf in the museum's warehouse.

"People who saw the movie *Bram Stoker's Dracula* might remember the scene of the woman who's buried in her Victorian wedding dress in an engraved glass box that's inside a stone vault," says Tina Oldknow, the museum's curator of modern glass. "But a real glass coffin was quite different. In fact, you might not even know it was made of glass because it's covered in doeskin that's embossed with leaves and flowers."

Oldknow says caskets like this were marketed in the late 1800s and early 1900s as being pretty and practical; once one was underground, nothing could get in—or out. "Our glass coffin was made in the 1920s by the DeCamp Consolidated Glass Casket Company of Muskogee, Oklahoma, and it came with a tube of silicone so that you could hermetically seal the lid forever," says Oldknow, who notes that although the company patented the product and licensed other factories around the country to produce glass caskets, it appears that few were actually made. Oldknow suspects that the museum's casket was most likely a funeral home sample. "Most companies claiming to produce glass coffins turned out to be fronts to attract investors and most investors saw no returns. So those companies quickly went bankrupt," she says.

While the Corning Museum of Glass does display a variety of glass reliquaries, including one that has never been opened, Oldknow says the glass coffin is never exhibited because "it's so big and it doesn't look very glassy." And, she says, "pretty much anywhere you put a coffin in a museum, it's going to make it look like a funeral parlor."

Corning Museum of Glass
One Museum Way
Corning, NY 14830
(800) 732-6845
www.cmog.org

CONTROVERSIAL FIREFIGHTER LITHOGRAPHS

FASNY Museum of Firefighting (Hudson, New York)

Built on the original grounds of the Firemen's Home of Hudson, New York, what is known today as the FASNY Museum of Firefighting first opened its doors to the public on Memorial Day, 1926.

Along with small objects such as banners and badges, the museum's first exhibit included four pieces of early hand-pumped fire apparatus in the gooseneck, piano, and double-decker styles, as well as a 1725 Newsham pumper, the oldest documented fire engine in New York state.

Today the museum, which is associated with the Firemen's Association for the State of New York (FASNY), has more than fifteen thousand objects relating to American firefighting history, including ninety pieces of firefighting apparatus and a wide variety of gear and equipment, fire service–themed fine art, photographs, and artifacts such as a bed key—a special tool firemen carried during the 1700s to quickly dissemble and carry off beds, which many colonists considered to be their most valuable pieces of property.

The museum is especially proud of its small but unusual collection of Fire Zouave materials, which relate to the Union army infantry regiment organized by Colonel Elmer E. Ellsworth out of the volunteer firefighters of New York City during the American Civil War. "They were considered the most effective men in the country," says museum collections manager Mary Zawacki, "and they had unique and colorful uniforms that were based on those of French colonial troops in Algeria."

Other exhibitions in the fifty-thousand-square-foot museum include a look at the science of fire, early firefighting equipment, the development of organized firefighting, and the role of firefighters in the 9/11 tragedy. But removed from display in 1997 for what Zawacki calls "rather controversial reasons" is a series of eleven lithographs published in the 1880s by Currier and Ives. Donated to the museum in 1962, the illustrations are part of a larger set of thirty-two from the "Darktown Fire Brigade" series that depicts African-American firefighters in a derogatory and racist manner.

"While such prints are considered reprehensible by today's standards, they do have historic value as they are indicative of an era and a culture very different from our own," says Zawacki. "During the time period they were published, lampoons depicting minorities or immigrants were cruel and demeaning, yet also very commonplace."

The lithographs had been on display at the museum for twenty-five years before being put away in response to sharp complaints from area civil rights leaders who called the pictures "insensitive and offensive."

Zawacki says that at the time, the museum had no professional staff to develop accurate interpretation for the prints. "Indeed, the prints were displayed with absolutely no context, leaving visitors with a disheartening and incorrect idea about the role of African-American firefighters." However, she says, "As an institute of public learning, the FASNY Museum seeks to interpret all aspects of firefighting history, no matter how distasteful. The museum

THE DARKTOWN HOOK AND LADDER CORPS.

Cultural sensitivities caused the FASNY Museum of Firefighting to put these Currier & Ives lithographs into storage. COURTESY OF THE FASNY MUSEUM OF FIREFIGHTING

hopes to include the prints in a future exhibit where we can interpret them in an appropriate context, exploring the important issues of prejudice, racism, and stereotyping."

For now, says Zawacki, "time and resources disallow such an exhibit," so the prints remain in storage.

FASNY Museum of Firefighting
117 Harry Howard Ave.
Hudson, NY 12534
(518) 822-1875
www.fasnyfiremuseum.com

THE DARKTOWN HOOK AND LADDER CORPS.
Going to the Front.

THE NEUSTADT COLLECTION OF TIFFANY GLASS

Queens Museum of Art (Queens, New York)

The work of decorative artist Louis Comfort Tiffany, son of Tiffany & Company cofounder Charles Lewis Tiffany, has fallen into and out of favor. But it's "in" for now, and the leaded-glass windows, lamps, furniture, ceramics, jewelry, and metalwork once designed and manufactured by Tiffany for public sale and private commission are highly coveted by collectors.

Tiffany's work is included in museums around the world, most notably at the Charles Horsmer Morse Museum of American Art in Winter Park, Florida, which houses what is said to be the world's largest collection of the artist's work and includes the rescued chapel interior Tiffany created in 1893 for display at the World's Columbian Exposition in Chicago.

Another major repository of Tiffany creations is the Neustadt Collection in Queens, New York, which was pieced together by dentist and real estate developer Egon Neustadt, who began collecting Tiffany lamps in 1935 and published an important book on the subject in 1970. The Neustadt Collection includes about three hundred Tiffany lamps as well as windows, metalwork, and many other Tiffany-made treasures.

Selections of the collection are displayed in touring exhibits around the country and in a small gallery at the Queens Museum of Art, but that represents perhaps just 1 percent of the Neustadt holdings. The rest is made of up of more than 275,000 pieces of the leftover flat and pressed glass used in the Tiffany Studios to make the intricate and colorful designs for which Tiffany became known.

And that cache remains in a warehouse in Queens, inaccessible to the public.

Louis C. Tiffany died in 1933 and collections director and curator Lindsy Parrott explains that in 1937, when the bankrupt Tiffany Studios was going out of business, the remaining stock—perhaps forty tons of glass—was offered up for auction. The cache of glass pieces now in Queens was part of that auctioned-off stock and it changed hands several times before being purchased by Neustadt in 1967.

While the majority of approximately 110,000 pressed-glass "jewels" in the Neustadt collection of Tiffany Glass are beautiful, they are small enough that they are difficult to exhibit in a meaningful way. COURTESY OF THE NEUSTADT COLLECTION OF TIFFANY GLASS, NEW YORK CITY

"The collection tells the story of both the incredible range of this beautiful material and the extraordinary challenge Tiffany's glass selectors faced when sorting through an immensity of glass to find just the right piece for the work at hand," says Parrott. "But while the majority of approximately 110,000 pressed-glass 'jewels' are very beautiful, they are small enough that they are difficult to exhibit in a meaningful way. They are really most impressive and meaningful when viewed as a whole."

Parrott says the same goes for the iridescent, or luster, glass in the collection. "A great number of pieces are what are often referred to as 'floor sweepings,' which are pieces of glass that are under one inch, and in some cases, measuring just about one-quarter of an inch," said Parrott. "Every piece of this glass is unique and very beautiful, but because the pieces are so small in size, and out of concern for the safety of the collection, it will never be shown."

Neustadt Collection Gallery
Queens Museum of Art
New York City Building
Flushing Meadows Corona Park
Queens, NY 11368
(718) 592-9700
www.queensmuseum.org

Neustadt Collection of Tiffany Glass
(718) 361-8489
www.neustadtcollection.org

KATHARINE WRIGHT'S KNICKERS

International Women's Air & Space Museum (Cleveland, Ohio)

Most people know the story of Orville and Wilbur Wright and their game-changing, twelve-second airplane flight over Kitty Hawk, North Carolina, on the morning of December 17, 1903.

Orville and Wilbur certainly deserve their place in aviation history, but they didn't get there alone. Although she didn't directly tinker with the planes or the plans for the planes, for many years Orville and Wilbur's younger sister, Katharine, served as a sounding board, social secretary, housekeeper, marketing manager, and ambassador for her brothers, making it possible for her notoriously shy brothers to attend to their aviation work full-time.

Katharine was sometimes referred to as the "third Wright Brother," yet her life story and her role in the birth and growth of aviation has been generally overlooked. But it is one of those told and celebrated at the International Women's Air & Space Museum in Cleveland, Ohio.

The museum was begun by women pilots and also tells the stories of Amelia Earhart, Bessie Coleman, Harriet Quimby, Jackie Cochran, and many others.

Memorabilia in the Earhart collection includes one of the pilot's flight suits, one of her nurse's uniforms, and more than sixty photographs of Earhart and her family and friends, donated to the museum by the pilot's secretary, Margot DeCarie. The Katharine Wright collection includes many items donated by the Wright family, including embroidered pillow cases, Limoges china, a strand of pearls, and a lace dickey. "We even have postcards that 'Aunt Katharine' sent from Germany when 'the boys' were visiting with Count Zeppelin," says collections manager Cris Takacs.

The museum also has the white dress Katharine Wright wore to accompany her brothers to the White House on June 10, 1909, when they received the Aero Club of America gold award. Included with that dress are the split-crotch knickers, or pantaloons, she likely wore underneath the dress that day.

The dress is displayed at the museum, but not the knickers. "If we were an Edwardian museum or a fashion museum, the knickers would be used in an exhibit," says Takacs. "However, we are a museum honoring the achievements

The International Women's Air & Space Museum has the dress Katharine Wright wore when she accompanied her brothers, Orville and Wilbur, to the White House in 1909, and the split-crotch knickers she likely wore beneath it. INTERNATIONAL WOMEN'S AIR & SPACE MUSEUM, CLEVELAND, OH

of women in aviation. We have flight suits, dress suits, a wedding dress made from parachutes, and various uniforms on display. But we would not think of putting [Wright's] underwear out on exhibit, since it would be connected with the story of an individual woman."

As far as she knows, Wright's knickers are the only knickers in the museum's collection and Takacs is a bit surprised the family kept them and sent them to the museum. "We have not displayed them, in part because there are still some members of the Wright family around," she says.

International Women's Air & Space Museum
Burke Lakefront Airport
1501 N. Marginal Rd.
Cleveland, OH 44114
(216) 263-1111
www.iwasm.org

NO ROOM FOR THE PIG

Rock and Roll Hall of Fame and Museum
(Cleveland, Ohio)

While there may be some hard work involved with educating the world about the history and continuing significance of rock and roll music, everything—and everyone—at the Rock and Roll Hall of Fame and Museum in Cleveland, Ohio, seems to just hum merrily along.

Eight permanent exhibits and several changing featured exhibits employ photographs, film, instruments, clothing, ephemera, handwritten song lyrics, and, of course, music to tell the stories of bands such as The Beatles, U2, The Rolling Stones, and The Who; individual artists such as Elvis Presley and Michael Jackson; and all manner of musical influences and trends.

The flying pig from the rock band Pink Floyd's onstage show is too large for the Rock and Roll Hall of Fame to fit in any of its galleries. PHOTO COURTESY OF ROCK AND ROLL HALL OF FAME AND MUSEUM. PIG CONCEPT BY R. WATERS

Among the special objects in The Beatles collection are John Lennon's Sgt. Pepper jacket, guitars, and other clothing and items played, owned, or worn by those crazy mop tops, and handwritten lyrics and drawings made by members of the band. A car and a jukebox that once belonged to Elvis Presley are here, as are Björk's "Post" jacket, some of Mick Jagger's stage outfits, and the Rolling Stones–themed pinball machine guitarist Keith Richards had and played with in his house. (The machine plays excerpts of Rolling Stones songs.) The Jimi Hendrix exhibit includes family photos, original drawings, guitars, costumes, original handwritten lyrics for "Purple Haze," and other artifacts. Along with memorabilia relating to Chuck Berry, The Who, U2, Metallica, and other iconic groups and musicians, the museum displays the signature white sequined glove Michael Jackson wore during the performance of "Billie Jean" on his "Dangerous" tour, along with the mask he wore for "Thriller" on the same tour and the jacket he wore in the video for the song. And for Janis Joplin fans, the museum has some of the singer's scarves and necklaces, her Porsche, and an undipped blotter acid sheet designed by Robert Crumb that bears Joplin's likeness.

The museum is also home to many of the iconic and oversize props used on the road by rock and roll bands during concert tours. "I think they add an element of rock and roll energy to the galleries," explains Jim Henke, former vice president of exhibitions and curatorial. Four cars from U2's "Zoo TV" tour hang from the ceiling in the museum's main lobby. The museum also has an eight-foot-by-sixteen-foot sign the group Weezer used on tour, and a huge hot dog that the band Phish used at a couple of its shows. A plane that Pink Floyd used as a prop on one of its tours hangs from the ceiling in the main lobby, but one of the well-known inflatable pigs the band had on stage for many years now remains off-site in storage because, at seventeen feet tall, fifteen feet wide, and twenty-five feet long, it's just too darn big to fit inside the museum.

"No other stage props we have are anywhere near as large as the pig," says Henke. "And as much as I like stage props, this pig is just too big to be put on exhibit inside the museum."

Rock and Roll Hall of Fame and Museum
1100 Rock and Roll Blvd.
Cleveland, OH 44114
(216) 781-7625
http://rockhall.com

"OLD SPARKY" CHAIR TOO UNCOMFORTABLE TO EXHIBIT

Ohio History Center (Columbus)

Museums and historical societies love to show off the items in their collections, but there are some objects staff members worry may be too shocking for the public to see.

That was the concern with "Old Sparky," the electric chair from the old Ohio Penitentiary that was first put into service in 1897, last used in 1963, and transferred to the Ohio Historical Society in 2002.

Designed, constructed, and built by penitentiary staff using what looks to be a dentist's chair of the time, the electric chair was first used to execute William Haas and William Wiley on April 21, 1897, and last used on Donald Reinbolt on March 15, 1963. Altogether, Old Sparky was used to end the lives of 312 men and three women.

Up until the early 1930s, Old Sparky was a highlight for visitors touring the Ohio Penitentiary and The Annex, where first hangings and later executions by electric chair occurred. (Souvenir postcards of the electric chair and of condemned prisoners were sold as well.) But when the chair arrived at the historical society, no tours were offered and Old Sparky went directly to storage.

"We talked about it for years, but we didn't display the chair because of the politics that still surround the death penalty in our state—it's still legal here—and because of all the hotbed issues of life and death, criminal justice, racial inequality, etc.," says Jackie Barton, director of education and outreach for the Ohio Historical Society. "It always seemed insurmountable to do it justice without overloading people or getting political."

The museum struggled with these concerns for years but ultimately decided that because the chair was part of Ohio's history, it could be displayed. "On their own, objects are neutral," says Sharon Dean, director of museum and library services for the Ohio Historical Society. "We give objects meaning by projecting our own memories, emotions, or prejudices onto them. And those meanings change over time."

With that in mind, the electric chair was put on exhibit for a short while in 2011 along with some other potentially hot-button, never-before-displayed

Altogether, "Old Sparky" was the tool used to end the lives of 312 men and three women at the Ohio Penitentiary. COURTESY OF THE OHIO HISTORICAL SOCIETY

items from the collection, including a sheepskin condom (circa 1860) found in the account book of an Ohio River steamboat captain, a wooden cage (circa 1870) used into the early part of the twentieth century as a restraining device for patients at a mental health facility in Cincinnati, a thumb mitt used to prevent children from sucking their thumbs, and a robe and a hood worn by a member of the Ku Klux Klan.

"The challenge was how to talk about these items without seeming to take a side," says Dean, who notes that the largest chapter of the KKK was at one time based in northeast Ohio.

Museum officials were unsure whether it was appropriate to display this wooden cage, circa 1870, used as a restraining device for patients at a mental facility in Cincinnati. COURTESY OF THE OHIO HISTORICAL SOCIETY

And although the staff wondered if police and extra fire extinguishers should be on hand for the exhibit opening, says Dean, "Putting those things out there was like ripping off a Band-Aid." In fact, the museum received notes thanking the staff for putting the items out, including one from a visitor whose grandmother had been murdered by someone ultimately executed in the chair and another from someone whose grandfather had been one of the people executed.

Ohio History Center
800 E. 17th Ave.
Columbus, OH 43211
(614) 297-2300 or (800) 686-6124
www.ohiohistory.org

JOHN DILLINGER'S GUN

Dayton History (Ohio)

John Dillinger is best known for a Depression-era crime spree of bank robberies, jail breaks, and alleged murders in the Midwest that transformed him from a petty criminal into an infamous gangster and folk legend. Books, movies, and TV programs have long depicted Dillinger as a nattily dressed gentleman bandit known for flirting with women during bank heists, chatting up reporters and prosecutors when in jail, and earning the title of Public Enemy #1 shortly after breaking out of the supposedly escape-proof Lake County Jail in Crown Point, Indiana, armed with a harmless carved wooden gun.

Dillinger's life and crime spree ended on July 22, 1934, at the air-conditioned Biograph Theater in Chicago, where he was trying to escape a heat wave. FBI agents waiting in the alley outside the theater shot and killed Dillinger as the movie let out.

This Colt .38 Super Automatic Pistol was taken from John Dillinger when he was arrested in 1933. The Dayton History Museum is concerned that it might get stolen if they put it on display. FROM THE COLLECTIONS OF DAYTON HISTORY

Death merely served to increase the crook's cachet. Souvenir hunters dipped hankies in his blood and later chipped away pieces of his tombstone. And today just about anything to do with John Dillinger remains a much-sought-after souvenir.

You can see a variety of Dillinger-related memorabilia, including his baby pictures, his lucky rabbit's foot, and that fake carved wooden gun (actually a replica of it; the "real" fake gun is so valuable that it is kept in a vault) in the John Dillinger Museum at the Indiana Welcome Center in Hammond, seventeen miles from the jail he escaped from in Crown Point.

But a very real gun he used in a robbery is part of a collection in Ohio managed by Dayton History, which operates multiple historic sites in that town, including Carillon Historical Park, a sixty-five-acre open-air history museum that's home to more than twenty-five exhibit buildings, the original 1905 Wright Flyer III airplane, Ohio's largest carillon, an invention-themed carousel, and many artifacts with a connection to Ohio.

Dillinger's gun—a Colt .38 Super Automatic Pistol, circa 1932—has a clear connection to Dayton history. It was taken off the bandit on the morning of September 22, 1933, when he was arrested in Dayton for a bank robbery that had occurred on May 10 in Bluffton, Ohio.

Etched into one of John Dillinger's guns is the date of his arrest for an Ohio bank robbery. He later escaped. FROM THE COLLECTIONS OF DAYTON HISTORY

"A few days after his arrest in Dayton, Dillinger was handed over to the Allen County authorities in Lima, Ohio, to stand trial for the robbery," says Gwenyth Goodnight Haney, community collections manager for Dayton History. "Dillinger's gang broke into the jail in Lima, freed Dillinger, and murdered Sheriff Jess Sarber in the process."

After that Dillinger and his gang went on what became a nearly yearlong robbery spree throughout the Midwest and West, ultimately killing ten men and wounding seven others.

While there is much memorabilia purporting to be Dillinger-related, the museum is confident the gun it has did indeed belong to the notorious gangster. Records show it being taken from him by a Dayton police detective and later brought to a local jeweler who inscribed this wording for the chief of police: "Taken from fugitive John Dillinger upon arrest by Dayton Police 2:30 AM Sept. 22, 1933—R. F Wurstner—Chief of Police."

The pistol was presented as a gift to Dayton Police Chief Rudolph F. Wurstner and donated to Dayton History by his family in 2004.

Mary Oliver, director of collections at Dayton History, says this connection and concern over being able to exhibit the gun in a secure manner are among the reasons it is rarely, if ever, displayed. "This is an artifact with immense historical value," she says. "Its provenance is impeccable," but "countering this incredible historic value is the fact that the topics that this artifact is associated with—crime and punishment—are not generally among the topics that we consider when planning our exhibits."

Oliver says the museum has considered incorporating the artifact into a future exhibit about the history of the Dayton Police Department but that ultimately the high possibility of theft due to the artifact's association with John Dillinger is what keeps the museum from putting the gun on display. "We value the artifact and the local and national history story that it helps us to tell too much to risk endangering it by placing it on frequent exhibit," she says. For now the gun remains housed in a secured, climate-controlled archive center somewhere in Ohio.

Dayton History
1000 Carillon Blvd.
Dayton, OH 45409
(937) 293-2841
www.daytonhistory.org

BATTERY NOTES TOO HAZARDOUS TO HANDLE

Chemical Heritage Foundation
(Philadelphia, Pennsylvania)

The Chemical Heritage Foundation (CHF) in Philadelphia, Pennsylvania, works to advance public understanding of chemistry and related sciences, and its museum is an intriguing educational showcase where some unique objects and exhibits help visitors understand the role of chemistry in our lives.

Temporary exhibits at the CHF Museum have ranged from the contributions of specific people in the history of chemical sciences to the creative and unusual ways in which artists interpret and depict the elements of the periodic table. The museum's permanent exhibits feature scientific instruments and apparatus (including three Nobel Prize–winning instruments), rare books, fine art (such as work depicting chemistry and alchemy from the seventeenth through the nineteenth centuries), the personal papers of prominent scientists, and artifacts such as a Nobel Prize medal and selections from the CHF's extensive collection of educational chemistry sets made for kids and sold by Sears, A. C. Gilbert, Chemcraft, the Smithsonian Institution, and others.

While the museum does not have a specific exhibit on the history of batteries, it does have in its collection documents and artifacts relating to the chemical processes and research involved with the development of these useful and, in many cases, essential items.

Hearing aids, pacemakers, toys, smoke detectors, and many other gadgets of modern-day society get their juice from small "button cells" or from those ubiquitous AA, AAA, and 9-volt alkaline batteries we now all keep at the ready.

But these everyday items would still be bulky, unwieldy, and unreliable had it not been for challenges presented by the walkie-talkies, wireless radios, and mine detectors used by soldiers during World War II and an independent inventor and scientist named Samuel Ruben (1900–1988) working in electrochemistry and whose research notebooks are now too dangerous to handle. According to Eric Hintz, a historian at the Smithsonian Institution's National Museum of American History, during World War II the US Army (via the National Inventors Council) asked Ruben to develop a new "tropical" battery that would perform better in the heat and humidity of the Pacific theater. "His resulting mercury battery was small, but powerful and long-lasting, and it helped power the walkie-talkies and mine detectors that enabled the Allies to win the war," says Hintz.

Ruben worked with the P. R. Mallory Company (later rebranded as Duracell) after the war on adapting his miniature "button" battery for a wide variety of commercial purposes, such as watches and pacemakers, and on the familiar alkaline batteries that still power radios, smoke detectors, flashlights, and many other products.

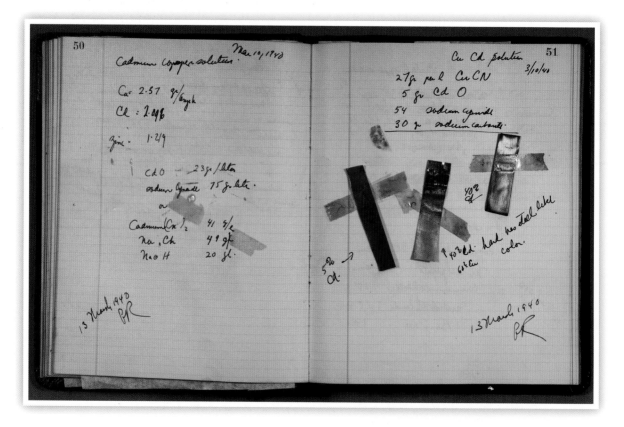

While researching smaller, better batteries, inventor Samuel Ruben taped his experiments into notebooks that are now too dangerous to handle. THE SAMUEL RUBEN PAPERS, COURTESY OF THE CHEMICAL HERITAGE FOUNDATION COLLECTIONS, PHOTOGRAPH BY GREGORY TOBIAS

Batteries produce electricity via an internal chemical reaction, and Hintz says Ruben's experiments involved finding the best chemical combinations of materials such as zinc, mercuric oxide, and cadmium. He says Ruben would tape samples of these materials into the pages of his notebooks, along with scraps of metal or chemical pellets and expended prototype batteries, alongside notes on their electrical performance. "Sometimes, because of poor design or construction, these prototypes became corroded or even exploded," says Hintz. "And Ruben might tape a corroded or damaged test cell to the notebook page to remind himself why he rejected—or at least needed to improve upon—a particular design."

While Ruben used his notebooks to keep track of his ideas and the results of his experiments, they were also an important record-keeping tool. "Each day's entry is signed and dated by a witness," says Hintz, "in case that day's work blossomed into something patentable."

Although Ruben's research notebooks are still intact and part of the Samuel Ruben Papers at the Chemical Heritage Foundation in Philadelphia, they cannot be displayed in the museum alongside the wide range of exhibits that explore the history of chemistry and the role science plays in the modern world. "Many of the expended cells taped to the pages are somewhat messy," says Hintz. "And like any old battery, they leak acid and have flakes of corrosion at the terminals." Some of the by-products of these chemical reactions can be toxic, which is why Rosie Cook, registrar and assistant curator at the Chemical Heritage Foundation, says the museum cannot display the notebooks in the CHF Museum and must limit researchers' time handling them.

Chemical Heritage Foundation Museum
315 Chestnut St.
Philadelphia, PA 19106
(215) 925-2222
www.chemheritage.org

Sources include: Eric Hintz, "Miniature Power," *Chemical Heritage* 30, no. 1 (Spring 2012): 8–9. The Papers of Samuel Ruben, Othmer Library of Chemical History, Chemical Heritage Foundation, Philadelphia, Pennsylvania.

POISONOUS ART

Penn Museum (Philadelphia, Pennsylvania)

The University of Pennsylvania Museum of Archaeology and Anthropology—aka the Penn Museum—was officially founded on December 6, 1887. Since then the museum has sent archaeologists, anthropologists, and ethnologists on more than four hundred research expeditions around the world, from which they brought back more than a million items for the collection.

That means museum visitors can wander among gallery exhibitions that contain treasures from the Near East, Asia, Central America, Africa, the Mediterranean, and the Native American Southwest. And in the Egyptian Galleries they can see no fewer than nine mummies and a twelve-ton red granite sphinx that is said to be the third largest in the world.

The rotunda that displays many of the museum's Chinese treasures is ninety feet in diameter and ninety feet high and is one of the largest unsupported masonry domes in the United States. And while there's certainly room in the rotunda for a sixteen-inch statue of Tung Fang-So dating from the eighteenth and nineteenth centuries, the museum does not display this object due to concerns about exposing staff members or the public to something made of realgar, a natural red sulfide form of arsenic.

The statue looks innocent enough, and according to Stephen Lang, the museum's Asian section keeper, when the statue was made people would have wanted to handle it because it portrays a Taoist sage associated with immortality and longevity. In the statue, both the bearded sage and his young attendant are shown holding peaches, a fruit that is associated with immortality as well.

"The idea would have been that as people handled the statue, a little bit of the realgar would rub into their food and they'd gain immortality by ingesting the substance," says Lang. But researchers have found that people who did this too often sometimes suffered heavy-metal poisoning and died instead.

The statue shown here was first displayed at the Penn Museum in 1917. But later, when the dangers of realgar became known and it was learned that toxic materials are created when realgar is exposed to light, the statue was put away and is now stored in complete darkness. "It's not like you'll touch it and die," says museum head conservator Lynn Grant. "In fact, in Victorian

This Taoist statue looks innocent, but is made from a form of arsenic that makes it dangerous to handle. UNIVERSITY OF PENNSYLVANIA MUSEUM OF ARCHAEOLOGY AND ANTHROPOLOGY, IMAGE #234233

times arsenic was an additive used in a lot of makeup. Society women would ingest a lot of it because it made their complexions clear and translucent. But today we take arsenic very seriously, so for the safety of the artifact and for the safety of the people around it, we won't be exhibiting it."

The realgar statue isn't the only dangerous item the museum keeps under wraps. Lang says early curators were interested in all aspects of a culture, so they sometimes collected arrows and other objects treated with poison. "We also have rhino (horn) libation cups that are said to be able to detect poison and some Duanwu Festival (Dragon Boat Festival) mandarin squares (embroidered badges) that depict the five noxious animals that ward off bad spirits. These aren't considered dangerous to touch but are related to poison and China." Lang says today museum staff make sure to label any object they think has been treated with poison with a "Fragile—do not touch" tag and use XRF spectroscopy to determine whether certain objects are potentially dangerous.

Penn Museum
University of Pennsylvania Museum of Archaeology and Anthropology
3260 South St.
Philadelphia, PA 19104
(215) 898-4000
www.penn.museum

Sources include: V. Daniels, "Chinese Realgar Figurines: A Study of Deterioration and Method of Manufacture," *MASCA Journal,* December 1983, pp. 170–172. Citing J. Needham, *Science and Civilization* 5, no. 2: 282 (London: Cambridge University Press, 1974).

WARHOL TIME CAPSULES

Andy Warhol Museum (Pittsburgh, Pennsylvania)

When artist Andy Warhol died in 1987, he left behind miles of film, video, and audiotapes, and thousands of paintings, photographs, and works on paper.

He also left behind a lot of what some would call trash.

Warhol was a hoarder who didn't like throwing anything away. So whether it was a phone message, a magazine, a newspaper, or a drawing on a piece of scrap paper, Warhol wanted to keep it.

Andy Warhol would periodically sweep everything off his desk into a packing box. A staff member would seal the box, date it, and send it off to storage to become a treasure-filled "Time Capsule." 97 OF ANDY WARHOL'S TIME CAPSULES, THE ANDY WARHOL MUSEUM, PITTSBURGH, 2012. COLLECTION OF THE ANDY WARHOL MUSEUM

That added up to a lot of stuff. And when it came time to move Warhol's studios from one building on New York's Union Square to another in the 1970s, a staff member mentioned that the hundreds of identical cardboard boxes being filled with Warhol's stuff could be considered time capsules.

Warhol latched onto that idea and declared it an ongoing work of art. And, after that, Warhol would periodically sweep everything off his desk into one of those same-sized packing boxes and a staff member would seal the box, date it, and send it off to storage.

Now, Warhol's 612 Time Capsules—mostly those cardboard boxes, but also some two-drawer file cabinets and one big trunk—are stored at the Andy Warhol Museum in Pittsburgh, Pennsylvania. Each box may contain multiple pieces of artwork, but each box is also considered an individual work of art. And, altogether, the 612 Time Capsules constitute a single piece of art.

No one knows for sure what treasures are in all those boxes, but since 1991 there's been a project underway to unpack the boxes and find out. The goal is to have each box opened, emptied out, meticulously cataloged, carefully repacked and then put back in storage.

Andy Warhol saved ephemera from his life in treasure-filled "Time Capsules," now in storage at the Warhol Museum. *TIME CAPSULE - 11*, 1977, COLLECTION OF THE ANDY WARHOL MUSEUM

Matt Wrbican, now the museum's chief archivist, was the first to start opening boxes and inventorying their contents. Early on, he found original artwork by Warhol, Keith Haring, and other artists; unopened bills from the surgeon who saved Warhol's life after an assassination attempt in 1968; hundreds and hundreds of invitations; old food; newspaper clippings; and even a pair of Clark Gable's shoes.

"The shoes were sent to Warhol by Gable's widow, who had read that Warhol was collecting celebrity shoes," said Wrbican. "We're not sure how he got actress Jean Harlow's gown."

Over the years Wrbican and a team of three catalogers have found plenty of other unusual objects and real treasures. While twenty to thirty of the Time Capsules are completely filled with newspapers and newspaper clippings saved, for some reason, by Warhol, the boxes have also yielded a mummified foot, a piece of cake purported to be from a birthday party for Caroline Kennedy, multiple sets of silverware and other items taken by Warhol and his travel companions from the French Concorde supersonic jet, and thousands of personal notes and letters.

Everything that's been taken out of the boxes has been put back, with a few exceptions. "The birthday cake and the pizza dough that filled one entire box were all crumbled and had to be documented and then thrown away," said Wrbican. "We also had to get rid of old batteries from cameras and exploded cans of soup and soda pop. Leaking batteries are dangerous and old food attracts pests. And you can't have that in a museum."

All of Andy Warhol's 612 Time Capsules are scheduled to be opened and cataloged by the end of 2013, but the boxes will still hold plenty of treasures and unraveled mysteries.

"There are different kinds of mystery and different ways of knowing what is in those Time Capsules," said Wrbican. "There are bits of correspondence and all kinds of objects that make you wonder why Warhol saved something and why it has significance. So while we may have cataloged everything, until researchers go through everything and discover the stories that go with each object, there's always going to be at least that much mystery inside these boxes. And that may take many more decades of work."

Andy Warhol Museum
117 Sandusky St.
Pittsburgh, PA 15212
(412) 237-8300
www.warhol.org

WREATH FROM ANDREW JOHNSON'S GRAVE

Andrew Johnson National Historic Site and National Cemetery (Greenville, Tennessee)

Rare Native American baskets, what may be the only remaining Sibley tent dating to the Civil War, and a daguerreotype of President Abraham Lincoln from writer Carl Sandburg's collection of Lincoln memorabilia are among the millions of objects and archived materials overseen by agencies of the US Department of the Interior. The collections are maintained by the National Park Service, the US Fish and Wildlife Service, the Bureau of Indian Affairs, the Bureau of Reclamation, the Bureau of Land Management, the US Geological Survey, and other Interior offices.

"The department owns and manages an estimated 170 million museum objects and archives," says Terry Childs, museum program manager for the Department of the Interior. "And only a fraction of those items are ever seen by the public."

Childs says the objects are stored in more than five hundred bureau facilities, including three hundred national park units, and in nearly one thousand nonfederal facilities, such as state, tribal, and local museums, university departments, and historical societies. While one of the department's goals is to make its museum collections available for research, education, and heritage activities by Interior employees, researchers, and others, there are a wide variety of challenges in making such a large number of objects and archives available for public viewing and access.

"Those challenges include the need for expensive conservation treatment on many objects, the need for scientific equipment to view objects that are microscopic, and the need for proper storage containers to help preserve objects," says Childs. "There's also the issue of insufficient professional staff and funding to create exhibits for the public and keep track of all the objects."

Some objects are important to conserve, but not much to look at. "Geological rock samples and petrographic thin sections come to mind," says Scott Foss, a regional paleontologist for the Bureau of Land Management. "These are maintained as voucher specimens for the verification of scientific results or for use in future research, but are rather boring to the casual observer. Clay samples, for example, are preserved as thousands of gray balls of clay."

As in many museums around the country, many objects maintained by the federal government on behalf of the public are just too fragile to take out of storage. For example, the Andrew Johnson National Historic Site and National Cemetery in Greenville, Tennessee, a National Park Service site, has in storage the original funeral wreath that was laid on the gravesite of the country's seventeenth president after his death on July 31, 1875.

An article about the funeral in the *Greenville Intelligencer* (a local paper that was coedited by Andrew Johnson's son and his grandson-in-law) noted that after the funeral, "a beautiful bouquet of white lilies and roses, held together by a white satin ribbon with the mottos *The People's Friend* and *He Sleepeth* was laid on the grave." The Johnson family held onto that wreath,

President Andrew Johnson's family held onto the wreath that was laid on his grave and passed it down from generation to generation. It is now too fragile to display. COURTESY OF ANDREW JOHNSON NATIONAL HISTORIC SITE

passing it down from generation to generation, and finally donating it to the National Park Service historic site in 1992. "The lilies and roses have long since faded and the wreath and the ribbons are now too fragile to display or to be exposed to the light," says Kendra Hinkle, a museum technician at the Andrew Johnson Historic Site. "But disposal was never a consideration."

Other objects may have cultural significance that requires the Department of Interior to assume additional obligations. For example, in 2002 the US Fish and Wildlife Service (USFWS) became the custodian of a feathered headdress that once belonged to Geronimo, a leader of Bedonkohe Apache who spent his last days as a prisoner of war at Fort Sill, Oklahoma.

The FBI had seized the headdress after thwarting an illegal attempt to sell it. Following the criminal case, the FBI turned the headdress over to the USFWS, as required by the Migratory Bird Treaty Act.

"Items like Geronimo's headdress are particularly important not just for their history but also because of what they might mean to a particular group," says Eugene Marino, chief archaeologist for USFWS. "Because Geronimo was a significant figure for many, especially American Indians, it follows that his possessions might also be considered significant."

In early 2003 the USFWS began a detailed examination of the headdress following the requirements of the Native American Graves and Repatriation Act (NAGPRA) of 1990. And after extensive consultation with pertinent federally recognized tribes, the USFWS issued a final report in 2008 and returned the headdress to a museum in Indian Country. Marino says the headdress is now "under proper professional care, but stored away with no plans for an exhibit at this time."

Andrew Johnson National Historic Site and National Cemetery
101 North College St.
Greenville, TN 37743
(423) 638-3551
www.nps.gov/anjo/index.htm

JOHN MURRELL'S MUMMIFIED THUMB

Tennessee State Museum (Nashville)

Although the 3,500-year-old mummy was brought to Tennessee by a sea captain in 1860, pretty much everything else on display in the sixty thousand square feet of permanent exhibits at the Tennessee State Museum in Nashville has a direct link to the history of the Volunteer State.

There are bones from a mastodon that lived more than ten thousand years ago, artifacts from Native Indian tribes, a two-hundred-year-old dugout canoe, a frontier cabin, and a Conestoga wagon. Daniel Boone's musket is here, as is a wide variety of Tennessee-made furniture, as well as Civil War uniforms, battle flags, and weapons.

In addition to the state's largest collection of quilts (more than three hundred), treasures in the collection include President Andrew Johnson's piano, the hat Andrew Jackson wore to his presidential inauguration in 1829, the quill pen used by President James Polk to sign the peace treaty with Mexico in 1848, and a $240 check issued by the Republic of Texas to David "Davy" Crockett's estate after his death at the Alamo.

And while this museum has more space for exhibits than many others, many special objects still remain in storage, including what may be the mummified thumb from the right hand of John A. Murrell, a notorious criminal who roamed Tennessee and along the Mississippi River in the early 1800s.

Although the digit has been at the museum "for some time," says museum spokesperson Mary Skinner, it is not on permanent display in part because there's been some dispute over whether the thumb is really *the* thumb or simply *a* thumb.

Skinner explains that Murrell was a minister's son and, as an adult, "was a bad person" who moved around Tennessee and up and down the Mississippi River pretending to be a traveling preacher. "But while he was inside preaching, his team of bandits would be outside stealing people's horses," she says. Murrell would also steal slaves and was eventually caught, put on trial, and sent to prison.

According to legend and a series of letters in the museum's archives, when Murrell died of tuberculosis, either while in prison or shortly after his release, his body was embalmed, mummified, and put on display at a state medical college. "This horrified his family, who appealed to the governor to get his body back," says Skinner. "But before the body was sent to the family, a student at the medical school cut the thumb off Murrell's body and later presented it to the Tennessee Historical Society."

Sometime later the Tennessee State Museum inherited the holdings of the historical society and the thumb came with the package. And so did many questions about the thumb's authenticity. While early museum notes state that the thumb was said to be "all that is left of this noted person," letters in the museum's files from as far back as 1916 note that "doubts have been expressed as to the genuineness of the relic."

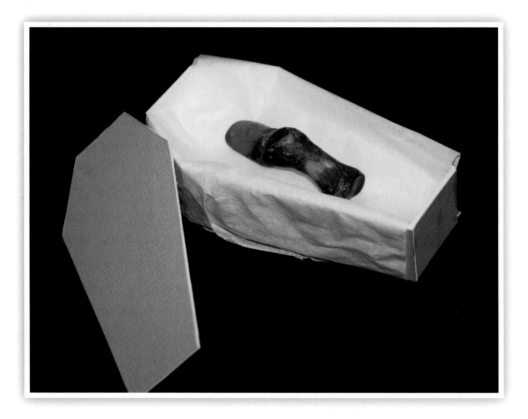

The alleged thumb of the notorious Tennessee bandit of the early 1800s, John Murrell. COURTESY OF THE TENNESSEE STATE MUSEUM

Skinner says museum officials are sure what they have in storage is a mummified thumb, but she says without any way of doing DNA comparisons on the thumb, they can't say for sure that the thumb they have is, without a doubt, Murrell's.

Either way, the museum is not going to let this thumb out of its hands. Although it's kept in storage, the thumb resides in a tiny casket a curator made for it.

"We take it out once a year," says Skinner, "during our annual Haunted Museum Ghost Story Festival Halloween event where we tell ghost stories based on local legends and lore."

Those stories include the tale of the Bell Witch, the ghost of a vengeful former neighbor who was said to haunt and taunt John Bell and his family in the early 1800s; of U'tunl'ta, or Spear-Finger, a Cherokee figure who was said to have a long, sharply pointed index finger and be especially fond of eating other people's livers; and of course John Murrell, the famous criminal whose thumb may—or may not—be one of the museum's most famous hidden treasures.

Tennessee State Museum
Polk Center
505 Deaderick St.
Nashville, TN 37243
(800) 407-4324
www.tnmuseum.org

POTTERY SHERDS

Scurry County Museum (Snyder, Texas)

The west Texas city of Snyder calls itself the "Land of the White Buffalo" and has a bronze sculpture on its courthouse square depicting the rare albino buffalo shot by noted buffalo hunter and rancher J. Wright Mooar near Deer Creek, in Scurry County, on October 7, 1876.

The Scurry County Museum notes that "the extermination of the buffalo was the single most important factor leading to the defeat of the Comanche and other powerful tribes of the Great Plains" and that during an eight-year span Mooar alone killed more than twenty-two thousand buffalo, sending many of the hides to his brother in New York, who sold them for $3.50 each.

Rare for its color, of course, the white buffalo has also long been considered sacred and spiritually significant to many Native American groups and is probably one of the reasons Mooar kept that unusual hide as a treasured souvenir. He displayed it in his home for many years and turned down many lucrative offers for it from prospective buyers including, the story goes, President Theodore Roosevelt, who offered $5,000, an incredible sum at the time, for the rare trophy.

The white buffalo hide still resides in Snyder, not in the museum, but at the home of Mooar's adopted granddaughter, Judy Hays. However, the Scurry County Museum has many other items that belonged to the famous hunter, including one of his coats, a pair of his hunting gloves, and one of the Sharps .50-caliber rifles that Mooar had specially modified so that he could hunt buffalo in the winter while wearing those gloves.

The museum's diverse collection of about fifteen thousand items also includes a quilt made with ribbons from the Grover Cleveland/Allen Thurman presidential campaign ticket of 1888, a section of a Columbian mammoth tusk, clothing dating back to 1870, a full leather shop with cast-iron equipment from the early 1900s, and a pump jack that can be activated by flipping a light switch.

Not on display, however, are the "finds" a local group of amateur archaeologists brought to the museum in the 1970s. According to museum curator Sarah Bellian, these items originated from what may have been up to seven dig sites all over the United States. "Though passionately interested in history, these amateurs incorrectly identified some of what they had found and left behind very little paperwork," she says. "They also used methods for excavation and restoration that were somewhat unorthodox."

Bellian says that for many years museum officials didn't even know that the amateur archaeologists' finds were inside the museum. But in 2010, when some new employees were reorganizing the collections room, they opened a cardboard box once used to store a water heater. Inside they discovered balls of yellowed newspaper that turned out to contain thousands of pottery *sherds* (the term refers to historic pieces of pottery) and five vessels that had been partially reassembled with masking tape. The person who had tried "repairing" the pots had long since passed away and was not available to help the museum sort out the pieces. "He had kept the sherds in brown paper bags

Amateur archaeologists used unorthodox methods of excavation and restoration (masking tape!) on a collection of pots donated to the Scurry County Museum.
SCURRY COUNTY MUSEUM, SNYDER, TEXAS

labeled 'living room rug' and 'kitchen table' and these bags did not contain just one single type of sherd. In some cases, pieces of one vessel were found in multiple bags," says Bellian, who estimates the total number of sherds to be about three thousand.

Bellian began researching and eventually identified the pottery as corrugated Mogollon red- and brownwares originating from either Arizona or New Mexico. She believes that the pottery sherds are between 800 and 1,500 years old and is confident that the pottery was made by tribes that lived outside Scurry County. The local resident who led the team of amateur archaeologists is now deceased and so can't help identify the exact location of the digs and, Bellian notes, "many laws have changed since the 1960s." So without knowing exactly where the pottery was found, the museum is unsure whether it can legally display these items. "If some answers could be found, we'd like to send these objects home to New Mexico or to a pottery conservation program," says Bellian.

Until then, the sherds remain in storage.

Scurry County Museum
6200 College Ave.
Snyder, TX 79549
(325) 573-6107
http://scurrycountymuseum.org

Sources include: *Snyder and Scurry County,* forthcoming book by Scurry County Museum.

CODED MESSAGE IN A BOTTLE

The Museum of the Confederacy (Richmond, Virginia)

Sometimes a museum treasure is hidden in plain sight.

That was the case of a message in a bottle at the Museum of the Confederacy in Richmond, Virginia.

Less than two inches long, the stoppered bottle has a .36-caliber lead pistol bullet inside as well as a slip of rolled-up paper tied with a linen thread. Put on exhibit in 1896, the museum's first year of operation, the bottle had never been opened, so no one knew for sure what was written on the paper inside.

But there were clues.

According to museum curator Cathy Wright, the bottle was donated to the museum by William A. Smith, a Virginian who had served as a captain

This coded message in a bottle was sent during the Siege of Vicksburg in 1863 and only decoded in 2008 by the Museum of the Confederacy and cryptographers. THE MUSEUM OF THE CONFEDERACY, RICHMOND, VIRGINIA, PHOTOGRAPHY BY ALAN THOMPSON

during the Civil War under General John G. Walker, the commander of a division of Texans nicknamed "Walker's Greyhounds." And back in 1896, Smith told museum staff that in 1863 the "medicine phial with lead sinker" had been sent to General John C. Pemberton in Vicksburg, Mississippi, but had never been delivered because by the time the delivery scout got to the Mississippi River, "Vicksburg had fallen."

Smith was referring to a forty-seven-day siege that ended on July 4, 1863. Weeks earlier, Major General Ulysses S. Grant's armies had converged on a crippled Vicksburg, which was then a strategically important town on the Mississippi River that Pemberton's armies had been trying to defend. When the Confederate troops surrendered Vicksburg, it was considered a major turning point in the American Civil War; at that time, Union troops had effectively captured the entire length of the Mississippi and cut the Confederacy in two.

So what was the message in the bottle?

Wright says museum staff had wondered about that for years. "It seemed tempting to tug on the white cotton thread protruding from beneath the cork, but there were curatorial concerns. The thread might snap; the cork could crumble; the bottle might break; the message could disintegrate."

Curiosity eventually won out. In August 2008 the museum had an outside conservator carefully open the bottle and remove the message, which was then unrolled by a paper conservator, photographed, re-rolled, and put back in the bottle, which was returned to display.

After all the waiting and wondering, here is what the message says:

July 4th
SEAN WIEUIIZH DTG CNP LBHXGK OZ BJQB FEQT FEQT XZBW
JJOY TK FHR TPZWK PVU RYSQ VOUPZXGG OEPF CK UASFKIPW
PLVO JKZ HMN NVAEUD XYF DURJ BOVPA SX MLV FYYRDE
LVPL MEYSIN XY FQEO NPK M OBPC FYXJFHOHT AS ETOV B
OCAJDSVQU M ZTZV LPJY DAU FQTI UTTJ J DOGOAIA FLWHTXTI
QLTR SEA LVLFLXFO.

Not surprisingly, the message was written in a secret code—but one that modern-day cryptologists could easily crack.

Translation:

July 4th
Gen'l Pemberton, you can expect no help from this side of the river. Let Gen'l Johnston know, if possible, when you can attack the same point on the enemy's line. Inform me also and I will endeavor to make a diversion. I have sent some caps. I subjoin a despatch from Gen. Johnston.

(Wright says "caps" means explosive devices and the "subjoin despatch" probably refers to a separate delivery that contained a key to help decipher the encrypted message.)

Lieutenant General John C. Pemberton had been desperately seeking reinforcements. But even if the message in the bottle had been delivered, it would not have helped. General Walker was not able to send help.

Cathy Wright says the scout sent to deliver the message likely got to the Mississippi River and realized Vicksburg had fallen. "What sparked this realization is unknown to history. Perhaps the absence of a Confederate flag upon the staff provided the clue, or an unusual sound—or silence—from the city. In any case, the courier did not toss the bottle into the river, for the lead bullet to sink into the muddy depths. He carried it back to Walker's camp and turned it over to assistant adjutant Captain Smith, who tucked it away, the contents not worth reading or the bottle not worth reusing—but luckily for the museum"—and now us—"important enough for him to keep."

The Museum of the Confederacy
1201 E. Clay St.
Richmond, VA 23219
(855) 649-1861
www.moc.org

Sources include: *Message in a Bottle,* talk by Cathy Wright, MOC curator.

SMALLPOX SCAB AND REDACTED LOVE LETTER

Virginia Historical Society (Richmond)

Founded in 1831, the Virginia Historical Society has a collection that has grown to include eight million manuscripts and more than fifteen thousand museum objects, including handcrafted objects made by early Virginia-based silversmiths, as well as muskets, pistols, swords, rifles, and other weapons made at a state-run manufactory in Richmond in the early 1800s.

The museum's long-term flagship exhibition explores 1,600 years of Virginia's history with more than one thousand documents and objects, ranging from a charred piece of corn cob thought to be about a thousand years old and the earliest known land survey done by a seventeen-year-old surveyor named George Washington to a one-hundred–gallon nineteenth-century liquor still and a window from Libby Prison, where up to 125,000 Union soldiers were confined.

The museum's available exhibit space has grown considerably over the years, but officials say the Virginia Historical Society fights the very same battle many other institutions do: not enough space to show off all the good stuff, many important but too-fragile-to-display items, and some objects in the collection that just don't fit into the stories being told in the modern-day changing or permanent exhibitions.

"It's not just a matter of space," says lead curator William Rasmussen. "We know viewers can only look at so much per visit. There is also the issue of managing the many objects in storage. It is easy to forget some, or just not know about things that came into the collection one hundred years ago or which may have not been displayed for a hundred years. They have all been identified accurately by diligent staff members; there is a paper trail to each and every one. But sheer volume is something of a barrier."

In June 2010 the museum took down that barrier for a short-term exhibition called *Bizarre Bits: Oddities from the Collection.* For the show, more than a dozen staff members were asked to put forth their favorite and most unusual finds.

Rasmussen says that among the more than forty hidden treasures put on display were objects that tell intriguing and unusual stories, were about odd people or events, or had an unusual color, shape, or purpose.

A chunk of tree fungus carved with the likeness of Robert E. Lee astride his beloved horse, Traveller, was "on loan" from a permanent exhibition in the

In 1857 Robert D. Minor sent this letter to his wife, Landonia, who kept the letters but snipped out the naughty parts. VIRGINIA HISTORICAL SOCIETY, MSS1.M6663. C1208

museum, but the first bullet to kill a Confederate soldier, silhouettes made by an armless Virginia woman using her mouth, a cigar found in a trunk belonging to Confederate president Jefferson Davis, and a bit of President James Madison's hair were among the treasures plucked from storage.

There were also two letters in the exhibit posted in the 1800s that included unusual enclosures.

The first is dated January 29, 1876, and contains the remains of a smallpox scab taken from a baby. "Honestly, someone would have thought it was a piece of dirt if it wasn't contained in this letter, because it was so small," says museum spokesperson Jennifer Guild.

William Massie sent the letter to his father in Charlottesville so that he could use the scab to inoculate his family members and friends from smallpox, which was a practice common in the day. A scab would be rubbed on or injected into the skin of a healthy person in the hopes of building his or her immunity to the illness.

The letter said, in part, "Dear Pa . . . Dr. Harris says . . . the piece I inclose is perfectly fresh and was taken from an infant's arm yesterday, but that you must let him know whether it takes & if it does not he will send you another scab—I am very sorry you lost the other scab, but hope that this will reach you in plenty of time."

The specimen was displayed encased in Mylar and, according to Lee Shepard, the Virginia Historical Society vice president for collections, was a great item to display because it not only was different and unusual, but also spoke to "the importance of disease, especially the smallpox, to early American and Virginia history."

While the scab was on display, the Centers for Disease Control and Prevention took notice: Before the scab went back into storage, the CDC "borrowed" the scab and took it to a lab at the agency's Atlanta headquarters to run some tests. It was returned to the Virginia Historical Society a bit smaller than before and sealed inside a test tube–like vial.

Another unusual letter included in the *Bizarre Bits* exhibition was sent by Robert D. Minor to his wife, Landonia, on April 26, 1857. As a lieutenant in the US Navy, Minor was away from home for long periods of time. In this letter he included fingernail and toenail clippings that, he informed his wife, he had kissed before putting them into the letter. He also included some graphic descriptions of what their reunion would be like when he got home.

Minor's wife kept the letter—and the clippings—but in what the museum describes as "characteristic Virginia modesty" she snipped the graphic sentences out of the letter, which was one of 4,300 pieces given to the Virginia Historical Society by the Minor family in 1948.

The historical society displayed the redacted letter in the *Bizarre Bits* exhibit but could not display the fingernail and toenail clippings because sometime in the 1950s a library assistant processing the papers decided that the clippings were disgusting and threw them out.

Virginia Historical Society
428 North Blvd.
Richmond, VA 23220
(804) 358-4901
www.vahistorical.org

TSA 9/11 ARTIFACTS

TSA Museum (Arlington, Virginia)

A small museum in Arlington, Virginia, houses some of the nation's most evoc-ative artifacts: a big chunk of subway rail recovered from the New York City subway station destroyed on 9/11 at the World Trade Center and the metal detector that screened hijackers Mohamed Atta and Abdulaziz al-Omari early that morning at Maine's Portland International Jetport. But unless you work for the Transportation Security Administration or have a special invitation to stop by, you won't be able to see these artifacts in person.

That's because the museum, which is called "Mission Hall," is inside TSA headquarters and is not available or designed for public tours. The exhibition space includes an interactive kiosk and a large, recessed exhibit case outside a multipurpose room on the first floor of the building in Pentagon City, a close-in suburb of Washington, DC. Only those who work in the TSA building or guests of the TSA can view the museum.

TSA historian Michael Smith says that's partly because his department has only two staff people, but that it's mostly because the main goal of the project is to share the history of the agency with the TSA workforce, which now includes more than fifty thousand people at more than four hundred air-ports across the country. "A lot of people, when you think about something like 9/11, they were just teenagers when it happened," says Smith. "So it's important to tell that story to all of our employees."

Smith was in a high school Latin class when the events of 9/11 began unfolding, and he remembers listening to news reports on a radio with his classmates and worrying about his parents, who both worked for the federal government in downtown Washington, DC (both were fine, and his mother later picked him up). In 2010, armed with a master's degree in history and experience working at several museums, Smith was hired for the newly cre-ated position of TSA historian. Since then he has been filming oral histories of current and past TSA employees, creating exhibits, and organizing a growing cache of objects related to the agency's history.

"When TSA first started up in January 2002 there were thirteen employ-ees," says Smith. "A lot of these people are friends of our project and had been holding onto documents, e-mails, coins, pins, you name it. Once they started donating those items to the project, the archives really started to come to life."

In 2011, to mark the tenth anniversary of the 9/11 tragedy, the TSA gave the Smithsonian Institution's National Museum of American History several artifacts relating to TSA history, including original TSA uniforms, some training items, and assorted pieces of aviation security technology. But Smith says hundreds of documents, artifacts, and digital remembrances remain in the TSA's own collection.

Among those items are images, oral histories, internal planning documents, a uniform, and other objects relating to the first airport to get TSA screeners: Baltimore/Washington International Thurgood Marshall Airport

The metal detector that screened the hijackers at the airport in Portland, Maine, on the morning of September 11, 2001. PHOTO BY HARRIET BASKAS

(BWI), which was "federalized" on April 30, 2002. "It was an exciting moment for the agency," says Smith. "This would become the largest mobilization of the government since World War II."

Limestone from the exterior of the Pentagon and mangled pieces of the World Trade Center are also in the museum's collection, as is an example of the first handheld metal detectors, or wands, used to screen passengers at airports, and the first American flag raised over Terminal B at Boston's Logan International Airport when the TSA starting screening there in 2002. Smith says the flag and that terminal are significant because American Airlines Flight 11 departed from Gate 32 of Logan's Terminal B on September 11, 2001.

And then there's the walk-through metal detector that screened the hijackers in Portland, Maine, that morning. Back then, private security firms contracted by the airlines were responsible for conducting airport screening, and all of the screening equipment was owned by the airlines. Smith says Delta Air Lines owned the Rapiscan machine the terrorists walked through in Portland, and after 9/11 the FAA pulled that machine off the line. "They investigated it and then the machine was put into storage by Delta Air Lines in Portland," he says. "It stayed there until 2005, when Delta contacted then–TSA administrator Kip Hawley and offered to donate the machine to the TSA."

That metal detector, complete with original identification tags used by Rapiscan, Delta, the FAA, and the TSA, is one of the items displayed at TSA headquarters in the *Never Forget* exhibit featuring artifacts from TSA's 9/11 collection. Smith says these objects illustrate stories about what happened that day.

"For our agency, 9/11 is what moves us and drives our mission. Putting the artifacts on display helps employees understand that mission because they remember where they were that day. They think about these artifacts. They think about what September 11 meant to our country. And then they dedicate themselves to doing the best they can every day."

Mission Hall, TSA Museum
TSA Headquarters
601 12th St. South
Arlington, VA 22202
www.tsa.gov
(Note: Not open to the public.)

MOON BOOTS AND SPACE SUITS

National Air and Space Museum, Smithsonian Institution (Washington, DC)

When men walked on the moon, they of course had to be specially dressed for the occasion. And they needed to be sure to wear the right shoes.

Sturdy boots were built right into every spacesuit, but NASA also issued each astronaut special overshoes, or lunar boots, that they were required to put on before venturing outside.

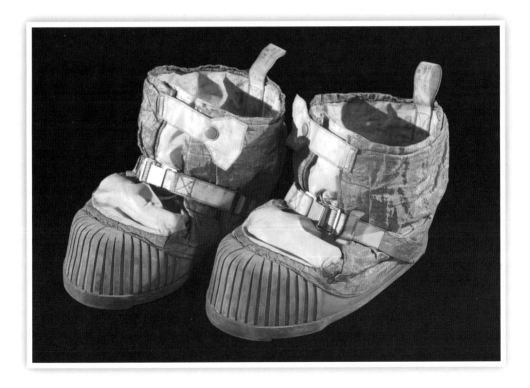

All astronauts who walked on the moon were supposed to leave their overshoes, or lunar boots, behind. The last two men to walk on the moon disobeyed and brought theirs home. PHOTO BY MARK AVINO, NATIONAL AIR AND SPACE MUSEUM, SMITHSONIAN INSTITUTION (NASM 2006-12210)

The boots—which created the footprint seen in the iconic photo documenting the first step on the lunar surface—have blue silicone soles and silvery woven stainless steel fabric uppers. "NASA chose silicone because they thought it would be the least sticky material; this was before Kevlar was available. They thought lunar dust would adhere to it the least and it would still offer traction on the moon's surface," says Cathleen Lewis, curator of international space programs and spacesuits at the Smithsonian National Air and Space Museum in Washington, DC. "When you think of something that sturdy, you'd expect them to be heavy like a work boot, but they're surprisingly lightweight and only weigh about five pounds each."

Still, due to overall weight and fuel considerations for the trip back to Earth, the boots were deemed too heavy to bring home and the twelve men who walked on the moon were instructed to leave their overshoes behind, along with a wide variety of tools and other equipment that would no longer be needed.

Two astronauts disobeyed those orders. Apollo 17 crewmembers Eugene Cernan and Harrison "Jack" Schmitt—the last two men to walk on the moon—decided to bring their lunar boots back to Earth.

"They made the decision between themselves while they were packing up to launch the lunar module back to the Apollo 17 spacecraft," says Lewis. "There had been certain advancements and they knew they had sufficient fuel and capacity and it didn't imperil the flight in any way."

The National Air and Space Museum later acquired the lunar boots from NASA and today displays just one pair at a time in the *Apollo to the Moon* gallery in the museum's National Mall building in Washington, DC. (The gallery is scheduled to undergo refurbishment.) "The boots are very precious to us," says Lewis. "They weren't supposed to come back. But they did. We weren't supposed to have them here on Earth, but we do."

While the Air and Space Museum has just two pairs of lunar boots, it does have close to three hundred spacesuits in its collection, as well as a wide assortment of spacesuit components and accessories. That includes spacesuits from the US and Russian space programs that have gone to space and back, as well as training suits and some developmental suits that have never flown.

Lewis says the crown jewel among them is, without a doubt, Neil Armstrong's Apollo 11 spacesuit—the one the astronaut was wearing when he became the first man to walk on the moon on July 20, 1969.

Like all spacesuits, Armstrong's outfit was designed to travel to the moon and back, to provide a life-sustaining environment for the astronaut in or out

Although Neil Armstrong's spacesuit was made to travel to the moon and back and to withstand extreme temperatures, it was not expected to last more than six months on Earth. PHOTO BY MARK AVINO, NATIONAL AIR AND SPACE MUSEUM, SMITHSONIAN INSTITUTION (NASM 2008-11302)

of the spacecraft, to withstand temperatures of plus or minus 150 degrees Fahrenheit, radiation, and the possible penetration of particles traveling up to 18,000 miles an hour. Lewis says the earliest spacesuits were very tough but, once back on Earth, proved to be quite fragile. "They were made right before the space mission out of materials that were available at the time and that scientists knew how to use," says Lewis. "The suits were meant for short-term use under very brutal circumstances and were made of materials that had a shelf life of perhaps six months, but that's all they needed."

Through careful conservation, and some trial and error, spacesuit conservators at the Air and Space Museum have been able to keep Armstrong's spacesuit, and many others, intact. Because the various materials used in each suit deteriorate in different ways, and at different rates, the solution has often been to disassemble the suit and store the parts separately under special conditions, in a specially built storage vault.

Neil Armstrong's spacesuit was displayed at the National Air and Space Museum almost continuously from 1973 until 2001 but was removed from exhibit and placed in the vault due to concerns about damage from humidity, light, the natural deterioration processes of the synthetic materials in the suit, the interactions taking place between components of the suit, and the fact that the suit had been upright for so long.

"It may go back on exhibit when we redo the *Apollo* gallery at the museum," says Lewis. "But if it does, it will be a in a very different display, under ideal conservation conditions, and in a special sealed case."

Smithsonian National Air and Space Museum
National Mall Building
Independence Avenue at 6th Street SW
Washington, DC 20560
(202) 633-1000
http://airandspace.si.edu

CONDOMS AND MARIE CURIE'S RADIUM

National Museum of American History, Smithsonian Institution (Washington, DC)

The iconic flag known as the Star-Spangled Banner, gowns and dresses worn by the wives of US presidents, President Abraham Lincoln's top hat, Muhammad Ali's boxing gloves, and the sparkly ruby red slippers Judy Garland wore in the *Wizard of Oz* are just some of the popular artifacts on display from among the more than three million objects in the collection of the Smithsonian Institution's National Museum of American History in Washington, DC.

A large condom collection is part of the health and medicine collection at the National Museum of American History. SMITHSONIAN INSTITUTION, NATIONAL MUSEUM OF AMERICAN HISTORY

Other exhibits explore everything from transportation, popular culture, and military history to technology and engineering, and each department has tens of thousands of objects that rarely, if ever, go on display.

Some are too fragile to take out of storage, but in the health and medicine department, which includes patent medicines, soaps, shampoos, toothpastes, syringes, eyeglasses, and all manner of medical devices, some of the items kept tucked away may be considered too controversial by some or may simply be too hot to handle.

While most artifacts from the museum's collection of condoms, birth control, and personal hygiene items aren't likely to be displayed, "those items are gathered as part of the museum's mission to build a historic record of material culture," says Diane Wendt, the museum's associate curator of medicine and science.

Wendt says some of the images on the condom packages are blatantly sexual, silly, or in bad taste and would definitely be offensive if included in an exhibit, but she notes that with the emergence of AIDS, the condom became a central tool in controlling a deadly disease. "Many public health groups and

This heavy, padlocked lead box contains a bit of Marie Curie's radium and is kept inside a safe at the National Museum of American History. SMITHSONIAN INSTITUTION, NATIONAL MUSEUM OF AMERICAN HISTORY

AIDS organizations package and distribute condoms, and the packaging now reflects the new role," she says. "So there's more thought in the design, which is often more sophisticated. The package also has an educational role, and thus some condoms have been included in a museum exhibit on AIDS."

The museum's health and medicine collection also includes a bit of radium that once belonged to two-time Nobel Prize winner Marie Curie who, with her husband, discovered the substance and its medical applications in 1898 but decided not to patent it.

As the price of radium soared, Curie ran out of her own supply to use in her research and studies, but in 1921 she came to the United States and attended a ceremony at the White House where she received a gram of radium ("a thimbleful," said the *New York Times*) that was purchased with $100,000 that a group of American women had raised.

Wendt says the Smithsonian has a bit of that radium, along with the vials and a frame used to display the remnants of radium Curie sent in 1903 to the American surgeon Robert Abbe, who is known as the founder of radiation therapy in America.

"A lot of people don't like using the word 'treasures.' But these are one-of-a-kind items associated with a very important milestone in medicine and science," says Wendt. "So in this case it works."

The Smithsonian has other items associated with milestones in medicine, including a sample of the original penicillin discovered by Alexander Fleming and vials containing residue from the earliest polio vaccines tested on humans by Jonas Salk. Wendt says those items could be displayed for the public, but with Marie Curie's radium, "there's a safety issue."

The radium is, of course, radioactive, so the vials stay inside a very heavy, padlocked lead box that has a sticker on the outside warning of the dangerous material inside. No one gets to see the padlocked box containing Marie Curie's radium, because it is kept locked inside a safe at the museum.

National Museum of American History
14th Street and Constitution Avenue NW
Washington, DC 20001
(202) 633-1000
http://americanhistory.si.edu

REPATRIATED WAMPUM

National Museum of the American Indian
(Washington, DC, and New York City)

The Smithsonian Institution's National Museum of the American Indian (NMAI) is dedicated to "advancing knowledge and understanding of the life, languages, history, and arts of Native peoples of the Western Hemisphere."

That's a tall order and a lot of territory. So it's helpful that the NMAI is actually two museums: the National Museum of the American Indian, on the National Mall in Washington, DC, and the National Museum of the American Indian–New York, in the historic Alexander Hamilton US Customs House in lower Manhattan. There's also a third facility: the Cultural Resources Center just outside of Washington, DC, in Suitland, Maryland, where the bulk of the museum's vast collection is kept.

The holdings include more than 825,000 items and represent just about every tribe in the United States and Canada, as well as many cultures from Middle and South America and the Caribbean. The collection is considered one of the most extensive of its kind and has at its core the collection of NMAI's predecessor, the private Museum of the American Indian (MAI) in New York City, which was filled with the Native American–related objects banker George Gustav Heye began amassing with gusto in 1897. Heye served as the museum's board chairman and director until his death in 1957, and the museum became part of the Smithsonian Institution in 1989, reopening in a new location, with a more respectful and definite Native American perspective, in 1994. (The Cultural Resources Center opened in 1999. The main museum in Washington, DC, opened in 2004.)

"So many natural history and other kinds of museums have put this material in an ethnographic category or looked at it as an outsider, from the perspective of anthropologists, archaeologists, art historians, and others," says John Haworth, director of the National Museum of the American Indian–New York. "And while we appreciate their perspective, this museum changed the conversation. Rather than an outside perspective, we look more from within the culture."

To that end, when museum staff decide how and whether to display something from the collection, they now closely adhere to cultural sensitivities.

"When the museum was the Museum of the American Indian, a lot of things were on display that should never have been on display," says Jacquetta Swift, repatriation manager for the National Museum of the American Indian. "We try to be as respectful as we can to cultural concerns and we usually err on the side of caution for the tribe."

The NMAI is especially mindful of repatriation issues and congressional mandates that require the museum to inventory and return human remains, funerary objects, sacred objects, and objects of cultural patrimony to lineal descendants and culturally affiliated Indian tribes as well as to Alaska Native clans or villages and/or Native Hawaiian organizations.

The National Museum of the American Indian recently repatriated one of the wampum belts in this 1871 photo. The wampum is a record of promises made after the War of 1812. NATIONAL MUSEUM OF THE AMERICAN INDIAN, SMITHSONIAN INSTITUTION, P09784. PHOTO BY PHOTO SERVICES

That means some objects that may have been in the collection for a long time are no longer available for exhibition at the museums because they have been returned to their owners and/or communities.

For example, in April 1999 a ceremony was held to return a hat in the shape of a bear to a leader of the Tlingit people in an Alaskan village. The Bear Clan hat, carved from a single piece of wood, had entered the previous museum's collection in 1907. Curators at NMAI's New York museum put the hat on display in 1994 in one of the new museum's three inaugural exhibitions.

Described as "glorious" and "magnificent," with abalone shell for the eyes and ears, and topped by twined spruce roots representing the clan's cultural patrimony, the hat had been used and displayed during the community's most important ceremonies but was removed under what the village and the museum later agreed were "questionable circumstances that invalidated the museum's title to it."

In an essay describing the hat's repatriation, James Pepper Henry, director/CEO of Alaska's Anchorage Museum, wrote that now the Bear Crest hat is "home in the Chilkat Indian Village of Klukwan, fulfilling its intended purpose as a proud emblem of the Bear Clan, providing continuity of tradition and history to future generations of Tlingit people."

In Canada, it's hoped that a wampum belt that in 2012 NMAI returned to the people of the Six Nations of the Grand River community in southern Ontario as an object of cultural patrimony for the Iroquois Confederacy (Haudenosaunee) will also fulfill its intended purpose.

On April 24, 1815, William Claus, Canada's deputy superintendent general of Indian affairs, gave the four-inch-wide, two-and-a-half-foot-long belt to representatives of a confederacy of indigenous tribes in Canada that had assisted the British in the War of 1812. "It includes Claus's account of the terms on which Britain had made peace with the United States, through the Treaty of Ghent," says Paul Williams, a member of the Haudenosaunee committee that works with museums on repatriation and other issues. "It accompanied Claus's assertions that the British would not have made peace with the United States had the Indian nations not been provided for," he says, "and includes rights to pass and re-pass the border freely."

Williams says this wampum, which is made mostly of purple shells with a design of white beads in what he describes as a "Greco-Roman zigzag" was not meant to be worn as a belt but kept as a record of a promise. And like similar records, it was to stay with "the wampum-keeper with other treaty and constitutional records, rolled up, in a bag, to be brought out and read on important occasions."

Unfortunately, when the keeper of this wampum died, it was sold by his children rather than being passed on to another keeper in the confederacy, and in 1906 it ended up in George Heye's collection and eventually in the collection managed by the National Museum of the American Indian.

In seeking the return of this wampum, Williams and his committee waited twelve years for it first to be located within the collection and then thoroughly researched and returned, a length of time Williams has found to be "average in term of things brought home."

But while this wampum is now kept in a secure, undisclosed location for safety, it is not kept from view. "Since its return, we've used it as part of an effort to get the government of Canada to take steps to fulfill promises made at the end of the War of 1812," says Williams.

"The museum looked after it, physically, so that it was not destroyed and did not fall into the hands of a private collector as other important wampums did. This wampum came back at the right time," he says.

National Museum of the American Indian
4th Street and Independence Avenue SW
Washington, DC 20560
(202) 633-6644

National Museum of the American Indian–New York
Alexander Hamilton US Customs House
One Bowling Green
New York, NY 10004
(212) 514-3700
http://nmai.si.edu

Sources include: James Pepper Henry, "Coming Home," in *Native Universe: Voices of Indian America,* p. 246, edited by Clifford E. Trafzer and Gerald McMaster. National Geographic Books, 2004.

SOAP MAN

National Museum of Natural History, Smithsonian Institution (Washington, DC)

The rare, dark blue, 45.52-carat Hope Diamond; dinosaur fossils that are millions of years old; an eight-ton, fourteen-foot-tall African elephant; totem poles; a squid that was once 330 pounds and thirty-six feet long; and the seven-foot-tall jaws of a prehistoric shark are just some of the iconic treasures visitors return to see year after year at the Smithsonian Institution National Museum of Natural History in Washington, DC.

The museum also boasts an insect zoo, a butterfly pavilion, a one-thousand-gallon aquarium, a hall showcasing more than three hundred mammals, and a gallery about life and death in ancient Egypt that displays coffins, mummy masks, human mummies, and the mummies of bulls, cats, ibises, hawks, crocodiles, dogs, and a baboon.

But even with a building the size of eighteen football fields, the National Museum of Natural History has room to display perhaps only 1 percent of its collection of more than 126 million natural-science specimens and cultural artifacts at any one time.

And among the treasures kept in off-site storage are the mummified remains of a man known as "Soap Man."

According to David Hunt, a physical anthropologist at the National Museum of Natural History, Soap Man was discovered in Philadelphia, Pennsylvania, in 1875, along with a soap woman and another individual during excavation for a train station in what would now be considered downtown Philadelphia.

Water had seeped into the coffins of the three individuals and, due to a chemical process known as saponification, the fat in their bodies had turned into a brown, waxy, soaplike substance known as adipocere, or grave wax.

After the soap people were found, Hunt says, they were sent to the College of Physicians and Surgeons in Philadelphia to be examined by anatomist Joseph Leidy. After that, the trio was split up: Soap Man went to Philadelphia's Wister Institute and Soap Woman to the city's Mütter Museum, where she is on display. "What happened to the third individual is not known," says Hunt.

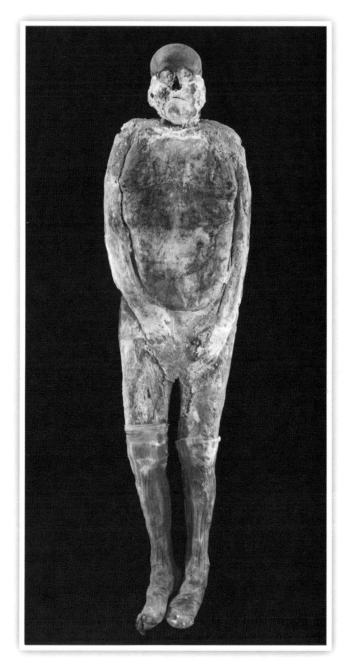

The Soap Man mummy was found in Philadelphia in the nineteenth century. Water had seeped into his casket, turning his fat to soap. © 2012 NATIONAL MUSEUM OF NATURAL HISTORY, PHOTO BY DON HURLBERT

In May 1958, Soap Man was transferred to the Anthropology Department at the Smithsonian Institution. His body was displayed from the 1970s until 1991 in the Physical Anthropology Hall in a sealed glass exhibit case with several other mummified human remains as part of an exhibit on human-body preservation. This display exhibited both naturally and culturally induced mummified bodies, along with Soap Man.

Hunt says that exhibit was closed down in 1991 due in part to new laws requiring museums to remove Native American human remains. "Soap Man was of European ancestry and for about a year and a half we had the exhibit up using only non-Native remains, but the administration decided to close down that hall anyway," says Hunt.

Since then some human remains have made their way back on exhibit. "Visitors really missed the mummies," says Hunt, and now human mummies from the museum's collection are once again included in the permanent exhibits about Egypt.

Human remains were also part of the museum's *Written in Bone* exhibition, most notably the skeleton of teacher, anthropologist, and noted Bigfoot researcher Grover Krantz, who asked that his body be used as a teaching tool by the museum after his death. Krantz's skeleton, along with the skeleton of his giant Irish wolfhound, Clyde, appeared at the end of the exhibit.

Soap Man, however, continues to reside off-site in a separate "dry" room next to the main physical anthropology storage floor at the Museum Support Center in Suitland, Maryland. The room has special humidity and temperature settings and houses desiccated human and animal remains from accidental and/or culturally induced anthropological and archaeology sources, as well as other items that require a drier environment for their preservation.

"We've considered getting Soap Man and Soap Woman back together at some point," says Hunt, "but for now in order for the National Museum of Natural History to display Soap Man, we'd need to have an exhibit that would let us tell his story in the proper context."

Smithsonian Institution National Museum of Natural History
10th Street and Constitution Avenue NW
Washington, DC 20560
(202) 633-1000
www.mnh.si.edu

STOLEN ART

Isabella Stewart Gardner Museum (Boston, Massachusetts) and Maryhill Museum of Art (Goldendale, Washington)

Sadly, there are some museum treasures the public cannot see—not because the items are too large, fragile, or controversial, but because the objects have been stolen.

That's why you won't get to see some priceless works of art by the likes of Rembrandt, Vermeer, and Degas, nor will you ever view two of the irreplaceable Indian Peace Medals distributed by explorers Lewis and Clark on their journey west.

The disappearance of thirteen artworks from Boston's Isabella Stewart Gardner Museum, in what remains the single largest property theft in recorded history, is now the stuff of legend. On the night of March 18, 1990, two thieves dressed as Boston police officers talked their way into the museum, tied up the guards on duty, and then proceeded to steal thirteen works of art from several rooms in the museum. Among the items stolen were three paintings by Rembrandt, one by Johannes Vermeer, another by Edouard Manet, and five drawings by Edgar Degas.

When they were first stolen, the value of the work was estimated to be somewhere around $200 million. But now the pieces may be valued at upward of $500 million. "It's not just the largest art heist in the world; it's the largest property crime in the world. And the more famous the work becomes due to its absence, the more valuable it becomes," says Geoff Kelly, a special agent from the FBI's Boston Division who works with the agency's art theft team. Kelly has been the lead investigator on the Gardner Museum theft for more than a decade and is confident the works will eventually be recovered.

"With the Gardner, the fact that more than two decades have gone by doesn't mean we won't get the work back," says Kelly. "Time doesn't really apply for these cases the same way it would with, say, a stolen vehicle. With paintings hundreds of years old it's not uncommon for them to be missing for quite some time before they are recovered."

For now, despite ongoing efforts by the museum, private investigators, and the FBI—which has offered a $5 million reward for information leading to the recovery of the artwork—none of the stolen treasures have been found. And today frames in the Gardner's Dutch Room, where many of the stolen works were originally displayed, remain empty, according to the museum, "as a reminder of the stolen artworks and their place in the museum and as a placeholder for their return."

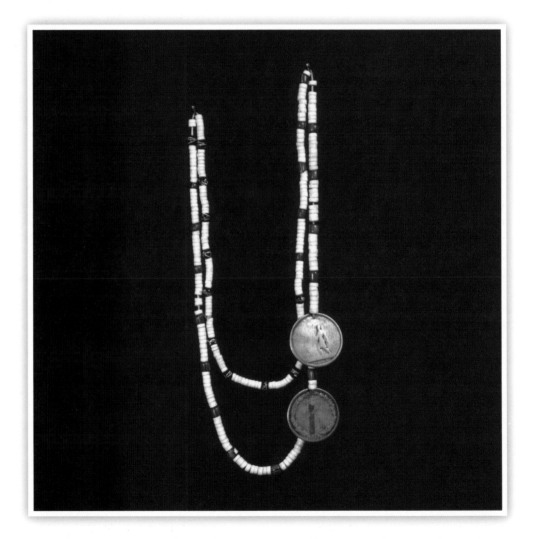

Meriwether Lewis and William Clark distributed these and other medals as tokens of goodwill on their 1804–1806 expedition out west. Not long after being put on display in the 1980s, these two were stolen from the Maryhill Museum of Art.
COLLECTION OF MARYHILL MUSEUM OF ART, GOLDENDALE, WASHINGTON

Less sensational, but equally disturbing to history fans and the museum broken into, is the disappearance of two of the medals President Thomas Jefferson gave to Meriwether Lewis and William Clark to take with them on their transcontinental expedition west and present to Native American chiefs as symbols of peace.

The medals that were in the collection of the Maryhill Museum of Art in Goldendale, Washington, were among the twenty-three (or twenty-four) medals noted in the Lewis and Clark journals and were known as Indian Peace Medals or Washington Season Medals because they were made for George Washington's second term and bore an image of a man sowing wheat. (Two others in the series depicted either a farm scene or a woman using a spinning wheel.)

The medals arrived at the museum in the 1940s and were most likely given initially to two prominent chiefs the explorers encountered as they traveled along the Columbia River Gorge. A direct descendant of one of those chiefs presented the medals to Maryhill.

When Colleen Schafroth, now Maryhill's executive director, came to work at the museum in 1986, she was excited to learn that the medals were in the collection, but surprised that they had not been exhibited for some time. She encouraged the staff to put the important local treasures on display but, unfortunately, shortly after they were placed in a special exhibit case, the medals were stolen.

"The case was broken into while the museum was open," says Schafroth. "It was noticed the same day, probably within an hour of the theft, but that is hard to say."

Shortly after this incident, the museum put in additional security measures. "We obviously can't display these objects because they are no longer here," says Steven L. Grafe, the museum's curator of art, "but we do hope to see them again someday."

Isabella Stewart Gardner Museum
280 The Fenway
Boston, MA 02115
(617) 566-1401
www.gardnermuseum.org

Maryhill Museum of Art
35 Maryhill Dr.
Goldendale, WA 98620
(509) 773-3733
www.maryhillmuseum.org

Sources include: *AWA* (Association for Washington Archaeology) *News* 5, no. 1 (March 2000): 3.

BAREFOOT BANDIT EVIDENCE

Orcas Island Historical Museum
(Eastsound, Washington)

Time magazine called him "America's Most Wanted Teen." And for a while he was.

During a multiyear crime spree that stretched from Washington state's San Juan Islands to Canada and the Bahamas and included dozens of burglaries and break-ins and the theft of cars, boats, bikes, and planes, Colton Harris-Moore, aka the Barefoot Bandit, was compared to everyone from D. B. Cooper and John Dillinger to Billy the Kid.

Heady comparisons for a baby-faced, troubled, over six-foot-tall teen from a dysfunctional family who escaped from juvenile prison in 2008 and then evaded police capture for two years. During this time he committed what authorities estimate to be more than sixty often-brazen crimes.

While on the lam he made his way into empty homes and took food, clothing, electronic gear, and credit cards. He broke into a bank, hardware stores, and markets, and in at least one store he allegedly left behind chalk drawings of bare feet and a message: "C•YA!" He stole boats and then beached them. He wasn't a trained pilot but prepared for flying the small planes he stole by ordering and reading pilot's manuals, watching instructional videos, and playing flight-simulator games. And he was finally captured in what was reported to be a "hail of bullets" in July 2010 after crash-landing one of those planes in the Bahamas.

For his crimes, Harris-Moore received a seven-year state prison sentence, which pleased many of the residents of Orcas Island, Washington. The Barefoot Bandit had spent much of his time on that island, terrorizing homeowners not accustomed to locking their doors, and bringing the FBI, SWAT teams, and police helicopters to a community many had sought out for being quiet and quite crime-free.

Orcas Island residents thought they were done with all that Barefoot Bandit business when Harris-Moore was captured and then sent to jail. But in November 2012 the local sheriff's office called the Orcas Island Historical Museum with an offer: Would they like to have the boxes of declassified evidence from the trial for the museum?

Colton Harris-Moore, the teenager known as the "Barefoot Bandit," stole small airplanes and taught himself to fly using video games and manuals he ordered online. PHOTO BY HARRIET BASKAS

"There was no hesitation," says Eirena Birkenfeld, the museum's former community outreach coordinator. "Our director immediately said yes. We were curious and interested to know what it all looked like."

But with the boxes of evidence came a post-bandit dilemma: Should the museum display objects related to a now-infamous crime spree or should it simply document the items and then hide away the evidence?

The museum, housed inside six relocated and strung-together homestead cabins from the 1870s to the 1890s, sits in the center of Eastsound, the island's main village. The story of island history is told through Native American artifacts and exhibits depicting early home life and local industries such as farming and fishing. There's also a display featuring some of the 110 ancient bison bones found in a peat bog on the island in 2008.

"Nothing in the museum is less than fifty years old," says Birkenfeld, "but the Barefoot Bandit story may change that."

Included in the first boxes of evidence delivered to the museum were the pilot's flight manuals Harris-Moore studied. "They were very moldy, so we wrapped them in plastic, sealed them, and I put them in my home freezer to kill the mold spores," says Birkenfeld.

The list of other evidence brought to the museum from the sheriff's office includes:

Two pot pipes

An iPhone in a red case

Chalk

Assorted screwdrivers

Crowbar

Wrench

Wire clippers

Harmonica

Folding knife

Bottle of aspirin

Black gloves

"There are also pages of handwritten notes on yellow legal-pad paper of plans and strategies, such as the best time of day or night to do certain things. Colton has very neat handwriting," says Birkenfeld.

At first the museum staff was cautious about letting the community know evidence from the case was on site. But then they decided to post a note on the museum's Facebook page asking for input on whether the items should eventually be displayed.

In reply to the comment asking "Why would you want to display items belonging to a felon?" one person wrote: "It is part of Orcas Island's history . . . which, good or bad, is reality." Another poster wished the museum luck with creating an exhibit that could certainly be a draw for tourism, but might offend locals who were victims of the Barefoot Bandit's crimes and had to deal with all the attention and fallout: "It's so early that emotions surrounding Colton Harris-Moore are sure to be very raw, but it IS a fascinating part of the Island's history and exciting for the museum to get the artifacts."

For its part, the museum staff is taking it slow, documenting every item in the boxes and in the many manila envelopes deputies have brought over in batches, and thinking carefully about how, and if, to share the evidence with the public.

Surveying the Orcas community about what to do has been considered. "But it might be a tricky thing to come up with the right questions," says Birkenfeld. "On the one hand is the fact that Colton Harris-Moore is now part of Orcas Island history. His presence dominated the island for many months. On the other side is the feeling that we shouldn't be giving him any more notoriety."

Orcas Island Historical Museum
181 N. Beach Rd.
Eastsound, WA 98245
(360) 376-4869
www.orcasmuseum.org

ROCK AND ROLL ARTIFACTS

EMP Museum (Seattle, Washington)

Seattle's Experience Music Project (EMP) Museum sits beside the iconic Space Needle and celebrates music, science fiction, and popular culture from inside a wild-looking, 140,000-square-foot steel and painted-aluminum building designed by Frank O. Gehry that takes its inspiration from a pile of broken pieces of electric guitars.

Inside the science-fiction museum, which takes up one part of the building, you'll find the Science Fiction Hall of Fame, which honors the lives, work, and ongoing legacies of science-fiction notables. Nearby you'll encounter iconic artifacts from sci-fi literature, film, television, and art, as well as an out-of-this-world parade of changing exhibitions.

This was Kurt Cobain's hat. Or was it? Museum staff aren't sure, so it is kept in the vault. KNIT CAP, CIRCA 1991, FORMERLY OWNED BY KURT COBAIN. EMP MUSEUM PERMANENT COLLECTION, GIFT OF WOODY MCBRIDE

On the music side of the museum, you'll find a towering sound sculpture that the Seattle-based artist Trimpin made out of five hundred guitars, banjos, and other stringed instruments, as well as a wide array of artifacts drawn from an 80,000-piece collection of music memorabilia relating to rock and roll and its influences on jazz, soul, gospel, country, blues, hip-hop, punk, rap, and other genres. In the Sound and Vision Library, the museum has a large collection of videotaped oral histories with key figures in film, music, literature, and science fiction.

A permanent gallery is filled with guitars from the 1770s to the present, including some invented by Leo Fender and Les Paul and others played by

The grunge band Soundgarden put many miles on this red van, which is too big to fit in the EMP's display area. CHEVROLET BEAUVILLE VAN: USED BY SOUNDGARDEN, 1986. EMP MUSEUM PERMANENT COLLECTION, GIFT OF KIM THAYIL

the likes of Bo Diddley and Eddie Van Halen. Changing exhibits also celebrate iconic musicians and groups, including many with Washington state roots, including Jimi Hendrix, Kurt Cobain, Quincy Jones, Pearl Jam, and Nirvana.

Among the items the museum doesn't display are a cap that may or may not have been worn by Nirvana's Kurt Cobain and a jacket and a vest that supposedly belonged to 1960s rock legend Jimi Hendrix. In both cases senior curator Jacob Murray feels that the provenance is sufficiently slight or cir-cumstantial that the items were important enough to keep, but just not quite worthwhile to display.

Another object the EMP isn't likely to display is a van that once belonged to Soundgarden, one of the key bands to emerge from the Northwest music scene. "It was the first band to be signed to Sub Pop, the first grunge band to sign to a major label, and the band everyone expected to be the first to break through," says Jasen Emmons, director of curatorial affairs. Emmons notes that Nirvana turned out to be the first Northwest band to hit it big, "but Soundgarden wasn't far behind and this is the van they toured in for years, loaning it out to other Northwest bands when they weren't using it."

For a while, the van could not be displayed because it did not fit through any of the doors at the museum. But Murray says that problem was solved when a doorway was widened to fit some *Battlestar Galactica* ships into the building for an exhibition on the science-fiction side of the museum.

"Even though we can get it in the doors now, there are some concerns about having a 'working' vehicle in an exhibition space, next to other fragile artifacts," says Murray. "And there may be weight issues in certain areas as well."

Still, he says, while the van is too difficult to display, "it's just too cool and historic to get rid of."

EMP Museum of Music + Sci-Fi + Pop Culture
325 5th Ave. N.
Seattle, WA 98109
(206) 770-2700
www.empmuseum.org

SWASTIKA AND KKK QUILTS

Yakima Valley Museum (Washington)

Horse-drawn vehicles ranging from a stagecoach to a hearse, a neon "garden" of advertising art, an extensive collection of apple box labels, and the reconstructed Washington, DC, office of one-time local resident Supreme Court Justice William O. Douglas are among the exhibit highlights at Washington state's Yakima Valley Museum.

The museum is also well known for its collection of more than two hundred quilts, the oldest of which dates back to 1805 and is made of a homespun wool and linen fabric referred to as "linsey-woolsey." These quilts were usually boldly colored in indigo, green, or bright pink and, according to the museum, were sometimes made from women's petticoats that were ungathered and flattened.

Due to the fragility of the fabrics and concern over colors fading, most of the museum's quilt collection stays in storage, and only select pieces are unfolded and displayed for themed shows. "The museum has a quilt-folding party every year to minimize damage," says Mike Siebol, curator of collections. "Studies show that rolling the quilts puts too much strain on them."

Two quilts from the collection that rarely go on display—but when they do, are shown together—illustrate how some museum-held objects are not at all what they seem.

One is a quilt top made in Germany for a young girl's hope chest that has rows of large red swastikas against a white background. The museum rarely displays this quilt in part because it is so fragile and because it elicits complaints from museum visitors even though the museum posts a label with large letters beside it saying, "This quilt is NOT a Nazi quilt" and explaining that, long before the Nazi Party adopted the swastika as its emblem, the image was a traditional symbol of good luck and hospitality in many cultures.

The other quilt is blue and white, looks pretty and innocent, and raises no initial alarms.

This quilt was made in 1928 by Mrs. C. C. Parmeter, the wife of a Puyallup, Washington, berry farmer, and has squares laid out in a curving, lattice-like pattern known as the Drunkard's Path. At the time, the pattern would have

Even though this quilt was made in 1914, long before the Nazis adopted the swastika symbol, it still shocks many museum visitors. YAKIMA VALLEY MUSEUM

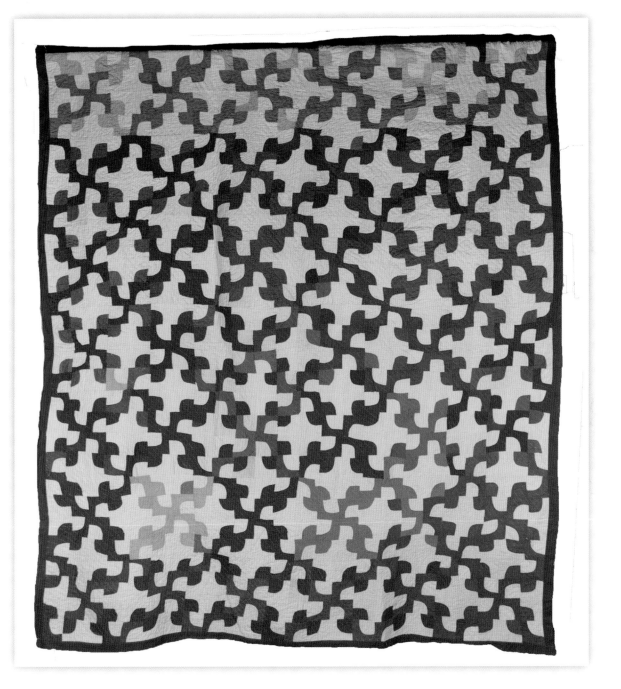

While this quilt looks innocent enough, the white fabric in it actually came from the masks of KKK robes. YAKIMA VALLEY MUSEUM

signified affiliation with the Women's Christian Temperance Union, which crusaded against alcohol and for women's rights.

This quilt was given to the Yakima Valley Museum in 1978, a decade after its maker died. The donor, possibly the quilt-maker's daughter, also left a note with the quilt that read: "You may not want to use this information but I shall write it down anyway, just in case you may want it. The white parts of the quilt were made from the masks of the robes worn by the KKK, or Ku Klux Klan. The state of Washington was teeming at that time with this organization. Some of the big brass of the police force in Puyallup were solid members and seemed to be the backbone of the lodge."

If not for the issue of fragility, Andy Granitto, the museum's curator of exhibits, would never put these two quilts away. "The 'Drunkard's Path' quilt, especially, tells such a wonderful story: 'Nice' families belonging to the clan; sweet quilt-making grandmas delicately hand-sewing Klan hoods into a sentimental family heirloom; the choice of the 'Drunkard's Path' pattern; and the eventual mysterious anonymous donation to the museum. It has everything you need for a great exhibit."

We'll never know if Parmeter used the fabric from the Ku Klux Klan robes in her quilt because she was trying to make some sort of political statement or—as thrifty artists surmise—if she was just making use of some perfectly useable cast-off materials close at hand. Either way, these rarely displayed quilts are a reminder that many museum-held objects have histories far more complicated than meets the eye.

Yakima Valley Museum
2105 Tieton Dr.
Yakima, WA 98902
(509) 248-0747
http://yakimavalleymuseum.org

HARLEY-DAVIDSON BEER, WINE COOLERS, AND CIGARETTES

Harley-Davidson Museum (Milwaukee, Wisconsin)

Whether it's stripped-down, straight from the showroom, or customized to the specifications of a finicky rider, a motorcycle gives its owner a nonconformist, at times "outlaw" or bad-boy/bad-girl image that Hollywood has happily embraced and enhanced over the years.

And while no one will scoff if you arrive in a car or a pickup truck, by bicycle, or on the bus, you'll definitely look and feel much cooler if you arrive at the Harley-Davidson Museum in Milwaukee, Wisconsin, on a motorcycle—preferably, of course, a Harley.

Although Harley-Davidson briefly licensed its logo to beer and cigarettes, "they're not products the company looks fondly on, in retrospect." COURTESY OF HARLEY-DAVIDSON ARCHIVES, MILWAUKEE, WISCONSIN

Wearing a leather motorcycle jacket might put you in the mood as well, but none of that is really necessary to enjoy museum exhibits that include more than 450 motorcycles and a wide variety of related materials spanning over 110 years and placing Harley-Davidson and the sport of motorcycling in the context of social history and popular culture.

In addition to galleries displaying motorcycles dating from 1903 through today, popular museum exhibits include the Tank Wall, which showcases many customized and iconic Harley-Davidson gas tanks, and the Engine Room, which includes a display containing an "exploded" view of all the parts of a 1940s Knucklehead model and another showing the evolution of the Harley-Davidson engine. There are also motorcycle-themed toys, motorcycles that visitors can sit on (and have their pictures taken on), and Serial Number One, a 1903 bike that is the oldest known Harley-Davidson motorcycle in existence.

Serial Number One sits inside an exhibit case that has a ten-foot-by-fifteen-foot line drawn around it representing the dimensions of the small wood shed in which the company was founded—and in which this first bike was built. Other notable bikes on display include King Kong, a custom bike that has two engines and is almost thirteen feet long, and a motorcycle purchased by a twenty-one-year-old Elvis Presley. "He completed his first recording session for RCA Victor, during which he recorded his star-making hit single 'Heartbreak Hotel.' He celebrated by buying a shiny red-and-white Harley-Davidson motorcycle," says curatorial director Jim Fricke. At the time, Presley was not yet rich and famous, so he bought the bike on time, with payments of $50 a month. On the paperwork, he listed his occupation as "Vocalist—self-employed." The Harley-Davidson collection includes the bike, the various legal documents detailing the purchase, and a set of iconic photographs of Elvis on the bike taken by photographer Al Wertheimer.

For true Harley-Davidson fans, the museum provides a "Steel Toe" tour that includes a visit to the nearby factory where Harley-Davidson engines and transmissions are made, and a "Back Roads" tour that takes visitors behind the scenes and shows them some of the items usually kept in storage.

But even those visitors don't get to see some of the museum's unusual hidden treasures.

That collection includes a variety of one-of-a-kind, experimental, test, and prototype vehicles documenting the development of both successful products and some projects that were canceled before going public. "Some we've been able to display in the museum, showing the product development process, but some remain off-limits," says Fricke, "due to proprietary technology or still-secret design ideas."

"We wouldn't encourage drinking and driving, or drinking and riding," says Jim Fricke, museum curatorial director. "Beer and cigarettes at least seem 'biker-like.' Wine coolers, less." COURTESY OF HARLEY-DAVIDSON ARCHIVES, MILWAUKEE, WISCONSIN

Over the years, Harley-Davidson fans have proven to be an enthusias-
audience not just for the company's motorcycles, but for all manner of
licensed products bearing the company's logo. Those items include clothing and accessories for adults, children, babies, and dogs, as well as Harley-
Davidson-themed Barbies and G.I. Joes, limited-edition guitars, jewelry, coffee
cups, and more. "We periodically pull some of this material from storage for
temporary exhibits," says Fricke, "but our primary exhibits deal with broader
topics of history and culture."

There are also some items bearing the Harley-Davidson logo, including cigarettes, beer, and wine coolers, that are rarely, if ever, displayed because "they're
not really products the company looks fondly on in retrospect," says Fricke.

Beginning in 1984, in association with some anniversaries and events, the
company licensed its name and logo for use on beer containers. "Each February there's a big Harley-Davidson rally in Daytona, Florida, and in August
there's one in Sturgis, North Dakota," says Fricke. "Lots of attendees drink
beer at those rallies, and someone decided to capitalize on the opportunity
to license the Harley-Davidson logo for 'commemorative' beer."

For five years (1988–1992) there were also Harley-Davidson branded cigarettes, and for a moment there in the mid-'80s the company also licensed
its logo for wine coolers. By current standards, says Fricke, these products
don't line up with the company image. "We wouldn't encourage drinking and
driving, or drinking and riding," says Fricke, "but beer and cigarettes at least
seem 'bikerlike.' Wine coolers, less."

Harley-Davidson Museum
400 W. Canal St.
Milwaukee, WI 53201
(877) 436-8738 or (414) 287-2789
www.h-dmuseum.com

ACKNOWLEDGMENTS

This book would not have been possible without the generosity and, in some cases, the bravery of the many museum staff members who enthusiastically, and sometimes very cautiously, agreed to share photos of and the stories behind some truly special objects in their collections. I greatly appreciate all the curators, directors, and community outreach people at museums who didn't let a book with the word "hidden" in the title scare them off; those who immediately "got it" when my initial call for nominations went nationwide; and those who were willing to open more drawers and closets in their storage areas when my response to their first (or second or third . . .) offering was "That's interesting, but what else do you have?"

I would still be trying to finish the manuscript, wondering if one more entry about very old food, naked people, or human remains is a good idea, and chasing down permission slips for all the great photos in this book, had it not been for Abby Rhinehart. She's a smart, calm, centered, enthusiastic, and detail-oriented young woman who showed up, genielike, at exactly the right moment to serve as researcher and release wrangler for this book. And she stuck it out with me to the end. Thank you, Abby.

Many thanks also to Erin Turner at Globe Pequot, who said yes to the idea of this book, twice. And to Courtney Oppel, who edited the manuscript and didn't seem to flinch when she learned early on that stories about museum treasures involving a mummified thumb, an electric chair, and body parts were on their way.

I've been on the museum beat for a long time now and want to thank Tom Cole, an arts editor at National Public Radio, who for many years guided me through many fun and offbeat feature stories about unusual museums and, later, through the more issue-oriented, twenty-six-part *Hidden Museum Treasures* radio project that led to this book.

Funding for projects on offbeat topics can be difficult to come by, but I am fortunate in that some of the radio features about museum treasures included in this book were made possible by grants from the National Endowment for the Arts, the National Endowment for the Humanities, the Corporation for Public Broadcasting, Humanities Washington, the King County Arts Commission, and others. Steven Lubar, now a professor at Brown University in Providence, Rhode Island, was a key adviser on the National Endowment for the Humanities grant when he was chair of the Division of the History of Technology at the Smithsonian's National Museum of American History, and his advice and his book, *Legacies: Collecting America's History at the Smithsonian,* remain touchstones for me.

INDEX

A

Abraham Lincoln Pole Banner, 43–45

Agnew, Spiro T., 54–56

Anastasiadis, Olivia, 11–12

Anchorage Museum at Rasmuson Center, Anchorage, AK, 1–3

Andrew Johnson National Historic Site and National Cemetery, Greenville, TN, 118–20

Andy Warhol Museum, Pittsburgh, PA, 115–17

Anonymous II skeleton, 68–70

Armstrong, Neil, 138–40

Arnold, Ken, 21–22

B

Bailey, William J. A., 79

Ball Jars Collection, 40–42

Barefoot Bandit (Colton Harris-Moore), 154–57

Barnum, Phineas Taylor (P. T.), 16–18

Barton, Jackie, 102

Bassuener, Kristy, 13

batteries and research notebooks as hazards, 109–11

Bauske, Clay, 72, 73

Bellian, Sarah, 124–26

Birkenfeld, Eirena, 156–57

Blaschka, Leopold and Rudolph, 60

Blood, Julie, 7, 9

Boca Raton Museum of Art, Boca Raton, FL, 14–15, 23–24

Bodle, Kelli, 14, 24

Burtsfield Elementary School, West Lafayette, IN, 41–42

C

Carpenter, Betsy, 68–70

Cernan, Gene, 138

Charles Horsmer Morse Museum of American Art, Winter Park, FL, 94

Chemical Heritage Foundation, Philadelphia, PA, 109–11

Children's Museum of Indianapolis, IN, 34–36

Childs, Terry, 118

condoms, 141, 142–43

Cook, Rosie, 111

Corning Museum of Glass, Corning, NY, 87–90

Cover, Stefan, 63

creepy things and live ammunition, 51–53

Culhane, Patrick, 65–66

Cultural Resources Center, Suitland, MD, 144

D

Dayton History, Dayton, OH, 106–8

Dean, Sharon, 102, 104–5

DeAndrea, John, 13–15

Denver Art Museum, Denver, CO, 13–14, 15

Dillinger, John and guns, 106–8

Drunken Monkeys Diorama, 65–66

E

Eichman, Shawn, 28, 29–30

Emmons, Jason, 160

EMP Museum, Seattle, WA, 158–60

Evansville Museum of Arts, History, and Science, Evansville, IN, 43

F

FASNY Museum of Firefighting, Hudson, NY, 91–93

Field Museum of Natural History, Chicago, IL, 31–33

firefighter lithographs by Currier and Ives, 91–93

Ford, Henry, 64–67

Ford, Linda S., 62

Ford Model T violin, 66–67

Foss, Scott, 118–19

Freemasonry, 57–59

Fricke, Jim, 166–68

Fricot Nugget, 9

G

Gardiner, Jeffrey, 59

Garfield, President James, 58, 59

Gasperich, Frank, 76

Geronimo's headdress, 120

Ghost Dance shirt, 46–48

glass coffin, 87–90

glass sea life, 60–63

gold jewelry, 7–9

Grand Masonic Lodge, Boston, MA, 57–59

Granitto, Andy, 164

Grant, Lynn, 112–14

Green, Karen, 77, 78, 79

Guild, Jennifer, 132

Guinness, Murtogh D., 80–82

H

half-heads preserved in jars, 37–39

Halter, Sarah, 37–39

Haney, Gwenyth Goodnight, 108

Harlan, James, 43–45

Harley-Davidson Museum, Milwaukee, WI, 165–68

Harper, Robert, 25–27

Harris, Neal, 16, 18

Harry S. Truman Library and Museum, Independence, MO, 71–73

Harvard's museums, Cambridge, MA, 60–63

Haworth, John, 144

Henke, Jim, 101

Henry, James Pepper, 146

Henry Ford, The, Dearborn, MI, 64–67

Heye, George Gustav, 144, 147

Hinkle, Kendra, 120

Hintz, Eric, 109–11

Hitler pin, 5–6

Hoffman, Malvina, 31–33

Honolulu Museum of Art, Honolulu, HI, 28–30

Horowitz, Mitch, 4–5

Houston, Melissa, 17, 18

human-skin wallets and scrapbook, 74–76

Hunt, David, 148, 150

I

In Cold Blood tombstones and gallows, 49–50

Indian Peace Medals, 151, 153

Indiana Medical History Museum, Indianapolis, IN, 37–39

inflatable flying pig, 100–101

insects, historically significant, 63

International Women's Air & Space Museum, Cleveland, OH, 97–99

invisible art, 68–70

Isabella Stewart Gardner Museum, Boston, MA, 151–52

J

Japanese woodblock prints, 28–30

jewels, pressed-glass, 95, 96

Jimmy doll, 52

John Dillinger Museum, Hammond, IN, 107

Johnson, President Andrew and wreath from his grave, 118–20

Jones, Trevor, 52–53

Jost, Stephan, 28–29

K

Kansas Museum of History, Topeka, KS, 49–50

Kelly, Geoff, 151

KKK quilts, 161, 163–64

L

Lancaster Country Day School, PA, 11, 12

Lane, Richard, 30

Lang, Stephen, 112, 114

Lewis, Cathleen, 138, 140

Lightner Museum, St. Augustine, FL, 25–27

Linda (sculpture), 13–14

Livingstone, David and medicine chest, 19–22

Loguda-Summers, Debra, 75, 76

López, Alma, 84–86

M

Malvina Hoffman Sculptures, 31–33

Marino, Eugene, 120

Martin, Kris, 68, 69, 70

Maryhill Museum of Art, Goldendale, WA, 152–53

Masonic urns, 57–59

Matchbox Flea Diorama, 34–36

McCartney, Kelly, 82

Michener, James A., 28–30

Minnetrista Heritage Collection, Muncie, IN, 40–42

Minor, Robert and Ladonia, 131, 132–33

Mooar, J. Wright, 124

Moomaw, Kate, 13

moon boots and space suits, 137–40

Morris Museum, Morristown, NJ, 80–83

Mozert, Zoë, 5, 6

Murray, Jacob, 160

Murrell, John A. and mummified thumb, 121–23

Museum of International Folk Art, Sante Fe, NM, 84–86

Museum of Osteopathic Medicine, Kirksville, MO, 74–76

Museum of the Confederacy, Richmond, VA, 127–29

music box and hidden clues, 80–83

Mütter Museum, Philadelphia, PA, 148

N

National Atomic Testing Museum, Las Vegas, NV, 77–79

National Museum of the American Indian, DC and NY, 144–47

Native American Graves Protection and Repatriation Act (NAGPRA), 47, 120

necklace, cursed, 53

Neustadt Collection of Tiffany Glass, The, 94–96

Nixon, Richard Milhouse, 10–12, 54, 56

Novara, Elizabeth, 54, 56

Nude Mozert painting, 5, 6
Nunn, Tey Marianna, 84–86

O
O'Grady, Christy, 34, 36
Ohio Historical Center, Columbus,
    OH, 102–5
Old Sparky electric chair, Columbus,
    OH, 102–5
Oldknow, Tina, 89, 90
Oliver, Mary, 108
Orcas Island Historical Museum,
    Eastsound, WA, 154–57
Our Lady Photo, 84–86

P
P. T. Barnum Museum, Bridgeport,
    CT, 16–18
Parrott, Lindsy, 94–96
Patton, Mary Elizabeth, 12
Penn Museum, Philadelphia, PA,
    112–14
poisonous art, 112–14
pottery sherds, 124–26
Psychiana Collection, 4–6
Purygin's Park of Recreation, 23–24

Q
Queens Museum of Art, Queens, NY,
    94–96

R
radiendocrinator, 77–79
radium and Marie Curie, 142, 143
Rasmussen, William, 130–31
redacted love letter, 131, 132
Released (sculpture), 14
repatriated wampum, 144–47

Richard Nixon Arm Wrestling
    George McGovern sculpture,
    10–12
Rock and Roll Artifacts, 158–60
Rock and Roll Hall of Fame and
    Museum, Cleveland, OH, 100–101
Rosado, Jose, 62

S
Sacco, Janice, 60
Saint-Pierre, Adrienne, 18
saltshakers, 26, 27
San Joaquin County Historical
    Museum, Lodi, CA, 7–9
Schafroth, Colleen, 153
sculptures, lifelike, 27
Scurry County Museum, Snyder,
    TX, 124–26
Sedona Heritage Museum, Sedona,
    AZ, 4–6
Shah, Monica, 1–2
Shapley, Harlow, 63
Shelley, Rowland, 63
Shepard, Lee, 132
shrunken heads, 27
Shunga (Japanese erotica), 28–30
Siebol, Mike, 161
Skinner, Mary, 121, 122, 123
smallpox scab, 132
Smith, Michael, 134–36
Smithsonian Institute, Washington,
    DC, 135–50
Soap Man and Soap Woman,
    148–50
Speegle, Clay, 67
Spiro T. Agnew Collection, 54–56
State of Iowa Historical Museum,
    Des Moines, IA, 46–48

Still, Andrew Taylor, 74

stolen art, 151–53

Stratton, Charles Sherwood (Tom
    Thumb), 16, 17–18

swastika and quilts, 161, 162

Swift, Jacquetta, 145

T

Takacs, Cris, 97–99

Tarr, Blair, 50

Tennessee State Museum, Nashville,
    TN, 121–23

Thomas D. Clark Center for
    Kentucky History, Frankfort, KY,
    51–53

Thompson, Jerome, 47–48

Tiffany, Louis Comfort, 25, 94

Trevillyan, Janeen, 4, 6

Truman, President Harry S. and
    portrait on the head of a pin,
    71–73

TSA 9/11 Artifacts, 134–36

TSA Museum, Arlington, VA,
    134–36

U

US Department of the Interior,
    118–20

V

Vincent, Karen, 40–41

Virginia Historical Society,
    Richmond, VA, 130–33

W

Wali, Alaka, 31–33

Walker, Thomas Barlow, 68

Walker Art Center, Minneapolis,
    MN, 68–70

walrus skull, non-radioactive, 1–3

Warhol, Andy and time capsules,
    115–17

Warren, Lavinia, 17–18

Washington, George, 58, 59, 130–33

Wayne County Historical Museum,
    Richmond, IN, 43–45

Weber, Captain Charles M.
    Weber, 7–8

wedding cake, 16–18, 27

Wellcome Collection, London,
    England, 19–22

Wendt, Diane, 142–43

white buffalo, 124

Williams, Paul, 146, 147

Wounded Knee massacre, 46, 47

Wrbican, Matt, 117

Wright, Cathy, 127–28, 129

Wright, Katharine and knickers and
    dress, 97–99

Wright, Orville and Wilbur, 64, 97

Y

Yakima Valley Museum, Yakima,
    WA, 161–64

Z

Zawacki, Mary, 91–93

ABOUT THE AUTHOR

Harriet Baskas is the author of a half dozen books, including *Washington Curiosities, Washington Icons,* and *Oregon Curiosities* (all Globe Pequot Press), and *Stuck at the Airport.*

She writes about airports, air travel, museums, and a wide variety of other topics for NBC News, USATODAY.com, MSN, *AAA Journey,* and many other outlets, and maintains two blogs: StuckatTheAirport.com and MuseumMysteries.com.

Harriet is an award-winning radio producer who for more than twenty years contributed regularly to NPR's *Morning Edition* and *All Things Considered* programs and most recently produced a documentary radio series about the one hundredth anniversary of Seattle's 1909 World's Fair (the Alaska-Yukon-Pacific Exposition) and the fiftieth anniversary of Seattle's 1962 World's Fair, known as Century 21. She has a master's degree in communications from the University of Washington in Seattle and served as general manager for three community radio stations in Oregon and Washington: KMUN, KBOO, and KBCS.